Social Finance and Health

Health systems across the world face multiple pressures. Input costs are soaring, systems are struggling to keep up with increasing demand for their services and areas of the world still lack universal health coverage. All of this whilst health inequalities between the best and worst-off within countries persist and, in some countries, are even widening. There is a need to think of new initiatives in response to these global health challenges. One such response is social finance.

Social finance is about creating social returns. This innovative and rapidly growing sector promotes new ways of banking and funding social and public services. However, social finance has an under-recognised, and potentially underexploited, role in responding to specific aspects of global health challenges: *funding* and facilitating *access* to health(care) services and *acting on* health. The objectives of this book are to conceptualise and evidence different forms of social finance – microfinance and impact bonds – acting in these ways and to critically engage with current debates and challenges. With such evidence to hand, we can either avoid adoption of new trends in financing public services or, more hopefully, attract greater policy support and resources for new tools for public health and in supporting more precarious, but potentially essential, parts of the finance sector.

This book will be essential reading to students, researchers, policymakers and the general public alike who are interested in, or who work in, and across, health systems and social finance.

Neil McHugh is a Reader at the Yunus Centre for Social Business and Health, Glasgow Caledonian University, Scotland.

Olga Biosca is a Professor of Economics at the Yunus Centre for Social Business and Health, Glasgow Caledonian University, Scotland.

Cam Donaldson is Yunus Chair and Distinguished Professor of Health Economics at the Yunus Centre for Social Business and Health, Glasgow Caledonian University, Scotland and Professor of Health Economics, National Centre for Epidemiology & Public Health (NCEPH), Australian National University.

Routledge International Studies in Health Economics

Charles Normand
Trinity College Dublin, Ireland

Richard M. Scheffler
School of Public Health, University of California, Berkeley, USA

Economics and HIV
The Sickness of Economics
Deborah Johnston

Medical Innovation
Science, Technology and Practice
Edited by Davide Consoli, Andrea Mina, Richard R. Nelson and Ronnie Ramlogan

Politics, Hierarchy, and Public Health
Voting Patterns in the 2016 US Presidential Election
Deborah Wallace and Rodrick Wallace

Equity and Healthcare Reform in Developing Economies
The Case of Turkey
Songül Çınaroğlu

The Digital Transformation of Healthcare
Health 4.0
Edited by Marek Ćwiklicki, Mariusz Duplaga and Jacek Klich

Social Finance and Health
Neil McHugh, Olga Biosca and Cam Donaldson

Social Finance and Health

Neil McHugh, Olga Biosca and Cam Donaldson

Routledge
Taylor & Francis Group

LONDON AND NEW YORK

First published 2024
by Routledge
4 Park Square, Milton Park, Abingdon, Oxon OX14 4RN

and by Routledge
605 Third Avenue, New York, NY 10158

Routledge is an imprint of the Taylor & Francis Group, an informa business

British Library Cataloguing-in-Publication Data
A catalogue record for this book is available from the British Library

Library of Congress Cataloguing-in-Publication Data
Names: McHugh, Neil, author. | Biosca Artiñano, Olga, author. | Donaldson, Cam, author.
Title: Social finance and health / Neil McHugh, Olga Biosca and Cam Donaldson.
Description: Abingdon, Oxon ; New York, NY : Routledge, 2024. | Includes bibliographical references and index.
Identifiers: LCCN 2023016353 (print) | LCCN 2023016354 (ebook) | ISBN 9781032304731 (hardback) | ISBN 9781032304748 (paperback) | ISBN 9781003305248 (ebook)
Subjects: LCSH: Medical care--Finance. | Medical care--Cost control. | Microfinance. | Bonds. | Health services accessibility. | Finance--Moral and ethical aspects.
Classification: LCC RA410.5 .M39 2024 (print) | LCC RA410.5 (ebook) | DDC 362.1068/1--dc23/eng/20230527
LC record available at https://lccn.loc.gov/2023016353
LC ebook record available at https://lccn.loc.gov/2023016354

ISBN: 978-1-032-30473-1 (hbk)
ISBN: 978-1-032-30474-8 (pbk)
ISBN: 978-1-003-30524-8 (ebk)

DOI: 10.4324/9781003305248

Typeset in Times New Roman
by MPS Limited, Dehradun

Access the [Instructor and Student Resources/Support Material]:
www.routledge.com/9781032304731

For Anna, Vaila and Finn

<Neil>

To the dream team: Alessandro, Alba and Iria

<Olga>

Diane, Graham, Callum, Dominic, Maisie, Freddie and Louie

<Cam>

Contents

Figures

Tables

Boxes

Part 1

Introduction

1 Social finance and health

Health systems across the world face multiple pressures. Input costs are soaring, systems are struggling to keep up with increasing demand for their services and areas of the world still lack universal health coverage. All of this whilst health inequalities between the best and worst-off within countries persist and, in some countries, are even widening. There is a need to think of new initiatives in response to these global health challenges; even in the presence of established welfare states and publicly funded healthcare systems. One such response is social finance. Despite being received in policy and finance circles as potentially transformational, more objective academic scrutiny of social finance has lagged behind. With a focus on health, this book aims to fill a large part of this gap.

While finance can solely be about money making money, as in the case of the financial markets, it can also be about creating a mixture of financial and social returns or, even, purely social returns. The value of finance, whether viewed as (un)ethical or having a positive or negative impact on society, is tied to how it is used. In recent years, the term social finance has come into popular usage as a way to collectively refer to individual forms of finance, such as microcredit, microfinance plus and impact bonds, that are concerned with achieving social and/or en-vironmental impact. While the 2008 global financial crisis acted as a stimulus for social finance, the idea of using finance to generate social impact is not new. The origins of social finance have roots in the work undertaken by (in)formal initiatives and institutions that have existed for centuries throughout the world to serve the needs of the most vulnerable, originally those worst-off in terms of income and wealth, in society.

Social finance represents a way of doing finance that responds to market failures and/or government concern for efficiency. Regarding the former, certain individuals, businesses and organisations struggle to gain access to financial providers or the types of finance provided are not suitable for their needs. For the latter, the concern is with using

DOI: 10.4324/9781003305248-2

resources in a way that maximises benefits and minimises costs. This is of particular importance in the context of fixed government budgets where resources are scarce and, if used in one way, cannot be used in another.

Forms of social finance can represent new ways of banking and funding social services, but their role in health and well-being enhancement, especially amongst the most vulnerable, has not been fully recognised, evidenced or exploited. On the one hand, social finance is new to the field of public health; it is not an obvious way to fund or facilitate access to health services or act on the wider social determinants of health. Likewise, much of the social finance sector would not perceive itself in the potential role of enhancing the health of its main client group; often the most vulnerable groups in society. Therefore, the objectives of this book are to conceptualise and evidence the role of social finance not only in *funding* and facilitating *access* to health(care) services, but also in *acting on* determinants of health, throughout the world. In doing so we will critically consider the prospects of different forms of social finance acting in these ways and engage with, and highlight, debates and challenges in adopting social finance for these purposes. With such evidence to hand, we can either avoid adoption of new trends in financing public services or, more hopefully, attract greater policy support and resources for new tools for public health and in supporting more precarious, but potentially essential, parts of the finance sector.

Focus of the book

Social finance takes a variety of different forms, including microfinance, impact bonds, credit cooperatives, social banks, venture philanthropy and crowdfunding (see Chapter 2 for further discussion). We will focus on two of the main forms of social finance – microfinance and impact bonds – that have the most developed links to health. Microfinance provision includes financial products, such as microcredit loans for business or personal use, microsavings and microinsurance, and (non-)financial services to individuals who cannot access mainstream financial institutions. Institutions providing these products are active across low-, middle- and high-income countries. Impact bonds are a form of Payment-by-Results that seek to leverage capital from private, philanthropic and/or third-sector investors to fund social and public services. The two main forms are social impact bonds (SIBs) and development impact bonds (DIBs). The main difference between SIBs and DIBs is the outcome payer; a government agency or body only (SIB) and an external third party, such as an aid agency, philanthropic foundation or charity, acting alone or alongside the domestic government (DIB). Our intention is not to suggest that these forms of social finance could solve global health challenges. We would be extremely sceptical of any single initiative or intervention making that claim. Instead, our aim is to explore the potential role of these forms of social finance in responding to specific aspects of such challenges: the *funding* of health and healthcare services (impact bonds), *access* to these same services (microfinance products and microfinance plus) and *acting on* health itself, especially that of the most vulnerable (microcredit and impact bonds). Figure 1.1 illustrates how these forms of social finance could stimulate mechanisms to positively impact the pillars of health (social determinants, preventive services and healthcare). Potential health impacts could occur directly through the funding and purchasing of, and access to, health services and community health initiatives or indirectly as non-healthcare and alternative public health means of acting on individual, community and/ or societal factors that are underlying causes of poor health. These conceptual links between each form of social finance will be developed and evidenced throughout the book and feature discussion of the potential challenges and negative impacts.

Importantly, we are not suggesting that social finance should replace all traditional financial instruments, particularly in relation to the funding of health and healthcare services. Rather, we are critically exploring how forms of social finance could complement their more traditional publicly financed and public health counterparts, leading to health creation in ways not often recognised. This necessitates the consideration of a number of outcomes such as impacts on health and well-being, access to services and the extent of funding and health(care) services available. While we generally focus on health impacts, at times we also refer to well-being. This is to acknowledge the overlapping nature of these terms and the importance of well-being for good health as well as vice versa. Beyond outcomes, we will also consider the wider consequences of these approaches by addressing issues around, for example, market-based responses to development and public service provision, alternative economic forms and measuring impact. As the stated health challenges are not constrained to one country or region only, we plan to take a global approach. This also aligns with the available evidence and will enable us to move beyond the more typical discourse of how the Global South can learn from the Global North to consider the antithesis, particularly in the case of microcredit.

Structure of the book

The crux of the book can be found in Parts 2 and 3. Part 2 features our 'Rethinking ...' chapters on '... finance' (Chapter 2), '... the funding of healthcare' (Chapter 3) and '... how to act on health inequalities' (Chapter 4). Chapter 2 sets out in broad terms what social finance is, where it emerged from and the need for it. Chapters 3 and 4, respectively,

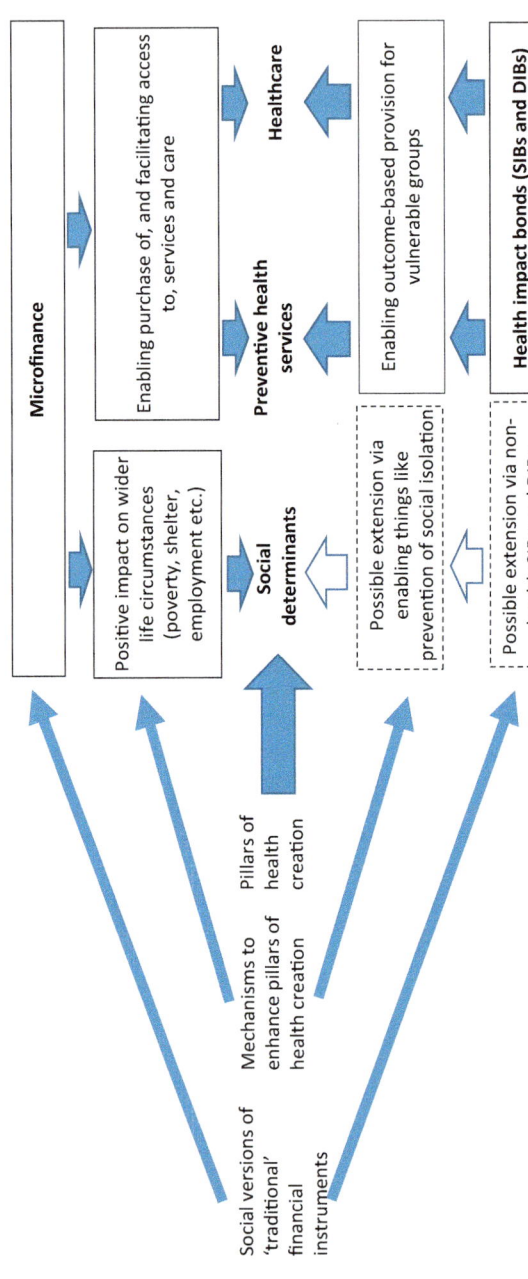

Figure 1.1 Social finance, health and healthcare.

discuss the typical ways of funding healthcare and the challenges facing these funding mechanisms, and why there is a need for other non-healthcare and alternative public health means of acting on health. These chapters provide the conceptual basis and set the scene for the third part.

Part 3 provides evidence and an in-depth discussion of the role of social finance in addressing global health challenges through our 'Social finance …' chapters on '… *funding* health(care) services' (Chapter 5), '… *acting on* health' (Chapter 6) and '… facilitating *access* to health(care) services' (Chapter 7). Chapter 5 focuses on impact bonds. Impact bonds are a new way to fund health(care) services and interventions and potentially act on determinants of health. However, we do not have a clear sense of their nature and reach in regard to health. After providing a general introduction to impact bonds and the arguments for and against them, we focus on a particular subset of impact bonds – health impact bonds. We present the results of a mapping exercise that provides a clearer sense of how many health impact bonds exist, where they operate in the health system, what they focus on and what indicators trigger payments. Chapter 6 is concerned with microcredit. Microcredit is typically viewed as a financial development tool to facilitate self-employment through business loans or consumption smoothing through personal loans. However, a nascent area of interest is the relationship between microcredit (itself) and health and well-being. After first introducing microcredit, we outline theory on mechanisms through which microcredit might impact on health outcomes and present evidence from low-, middle- and high-income countries with respect to such relationships. Finally, Chapter 7 is on microfinance plus. Microfinance institutions (MFIs) can offer a variety of financial products, such as microinsurance that can facilitate access to health(care) services. Similarly, MFIs, particularly in low- and middle-income countries, can directly provide or integrate with health(care) providers to facilitate access to health education (e.g. HIV training), health services (e.g. basic health screenings) and health products (e.g. medicines). This chapter discusses evidence and debates around this more-instrumental, direct relationship between microfinance and health.

Finally in Chapter 8 we summarise the role of social finance *funding* and facilitating *access* to health(care) services, and *acting on* health. While social finance has the ability to act in these ways, currently, it does so with differing degrees of success. Nonetheless, exploring the potential role of forms of social finance in responding to specific aspects of global health challenges generates new thinking and evidence relevant to those operating in health systems and social finance, and those trying to bridge the gap between them. We finish the book by outlining the new tools for action for policymakers, practitioners and researchers working in, and across, health systems and social finance generated from exploring social finance acting in these ways and contribute to debates around impact measurement.

How to read the book

Our obvious hope is that all readers will enjoy the book from cover to cover. However, as we focus on a number of distinct areas – microcredit, microfinance plus, impact bonds, healthcare and public health – readers may want to focus on aspects of the book that align with their interests. Thus, it is possible to read the book in three different ways. First, the traditional reader going cover to cover is self-explanatory. Second, readers only interested in microfinance could avoid Chapter 5 and those only interested in impact bonds may skip Chapters 6 and 7. Lastly, readers with an interest in healthcare could miss out on Chapters 4 and 6. For readers with an interest in public health, we optimistically think there is something appealing in every chapter.

Exploring the role of social finance in addressing global health challenges is a relatively new area of research. Much of this book emerges from a body of work undertaken by ourselves and other colleagues at the Yunus Centre for Social Business and Health, Glasgow Caledonian University, over a number of years. That work, like this book, is very much a collaborative effort. We aim to complement and supplement this work with the most up-to-date evidence and discussion of the possible relationships between social finance and health from the literature. However, what we have written is not definitive. Instead, we would encourage readers to see this book as a starting point. As will become clear, there is plenty of scope for new exploration in this area. We hope that however you chose to read the book you enjoy it and that it helps you identify new questions and ways to address the challenges facing health systems throughout the world.

Part 2

Conceptual basis

2 Rethinking ... finance

Introduction

Have you ever given or received money to help buy a house, a car, a school uniform, a new pair of shoes or get to the next payday? Have you ever put money aside in a safe place, whether a bank account or a drawer in your house, for some future use? Have you ever tried to raise money to establish or expand a business or to help your business through a difficult time? If the answer is yes to any of these questions, then you have engaged with some form of finance. While we tend to think about finance as involving (big) businesses, banks and money, financial exchanges are diverse and happen in our everyday life and social relations among family and friends. Frequently these are monetary exchanges but can also include non-monetary exchanges through, for example, time banks, gifts and the provision of care. Finance simply refers to the processes and instruments that individuals, businesses and institutions use to save, invest, lend and borrow. While finance can solely be about money making money, as in the case of the financial markets, it can also be about creating a mixture of financial and social returns or purely social returns. The value of finance, whether viewed as (un)ethical or having a positive or negative impact on society, is tied to how it is used. In recent years, a specific conceptualisation of finance – social finance – has emerged to differentiate and categorise particular forms of finance that are concerned with non-financial returns.

In this chapter, we introduce social finance and explain why there is a need for it. In doing so, we will outline the broad components of the social finance sector and provide an overview of the main forms of social finance.

What is social finance?

Social finance, in its simplest sense, refers to the provision of capital through market and nonmarket institutions, initiatives and financial mechanisms for social and/or environmental returns alone or alongside financial returns. The social and/or environmental impact created by the

DOI: 10.4324/9781003305248-4

recipients of social finance can occur in a variety of ways. For example, through the goods and services produced; the structure, processes, ethos and/or mission of a business or organisation; the target market or where the organisation is located; and/or the characteristics of employees or service users (1).

Social finance closely relates to 'social investment' (see Box 2.1). However, the latter is narrower, being concerned with the investment of capital only to generate social and/or environmental returns alongside financial returns (1,2). Social finance encompasses a wider range of capital types, such as grants, investment logics and investor rationalities (see Nicholls (3)), and risk return considerations than social investment (1,4). Rather than being viewed as "just a new set of 'social' capital return opportunities", the developing field of social finance is positioned by some as an alternative to the mainstream financial system as it seeks to overcome market failures (1, p. 3, 5) (see 'Why is there a need for social finance?')'. However, there is limited work exploring the alterity of the social finance sector in general and of specific forms of social finance, with exceptions being credit unions (6,7) and microcredit for enterprise in the UK (8).

Social finance acts as an overarching term that encapsulates a wide variety of capital and funding models, such as grants, debt, equity and quasi-equity, which are supplied or demanded by a variety of stake-holders, including individuals, businesses, organisations and governments (see Box 2.1). Intermediaries, who can supply or demand types of social finance and facilitate relationships between different stakeholders, also play a key role in the social finance sector. A wide range of social finance institutions and mechanisms also exist, including microfinance institutions that offer a wide range of financial products and non-financial services, credit cooperatives, social banks, impact bonds, venture philanthropy and crowdfunding. While this book primarily focuses on market institutions and financial mechanisms, there is a rich history and continuing presence of nonmarket and informal social finance initiatives and mechanisms in communities throughout the world (see 'A (brief) history of social finance' for an overview).

It is difficult to provide a clear sense of the size of the sector, as social finance is a fuzzy concept. For example, a for-profit bank could create social impact through private investments (4). However, we can gain some insight of its scale by considering estimates of various components of the social finance sector. Estimates of the size of the global market for microfinance in 2022 are $186.4 billion, with growth projections of approximately $304.3 billion by 2026 (9). The more recently developed impact bond sector has raised approximately $462.68 million dollars in upfront capital for the funding of interventions across the world and is growing year on year (10). While, in 2020, the Global Impact Investing Network (GIIN) (11) estimated the impact investing market size at $715 billion and the International Finance Corporation (IFC) (12) estimated that figure could be as high as $2.1 trillion for assets under management. A lower figure of $505 billion is quoted for assets measured for impact. These figures indicate significant growth in the impact investing market over the last ten years as, for example, the Global Sustainable Investment Alliance (13) estimated its market size at $89 billion in 2012. What is less clear is the size of the social finance sector around grants and philanthropic donations that do not require a financial return and the extent of social finance provision through nonmarket initiatives and mechanisms. However, what is clear is that the overall picture of the social finance sector is one of growth.

Box 2.1   Glossary of social finance terms

Overarching terms

Social finance: the provision (allocation or investment) of capital through market and nonmarket institutions, initiatives and financial mechanisms for social and/or environmental returns alone or alongside financial returns.

Social investment: the investment of capital to generate social and/or environmental returns alongside financial returns.

Capital: money or other assets individuals or organisations allocate to, or invest in, other individuals/organisations.

Types of social finance

Grants: allocated money with no repayment requirement. This money does not generate a return for the grantor.

Debt: borrowed money for personal or business purposes with a repayment requirement, typically but not always, with interest.

Equity: selling shares in a business or company to raise money.

Quasi-equity: selling a right to a percentage share of future revenue (not profit) in a business or company to raise money.

Social finance structure

Supply: individuals, institutions, organisations or governments that allocate or invest different forms of capital to generate social and/or environmental returns either alone or alongside financial returns.

Demand: recipients, such as in individuals, businesses or organisations, of different types of social finance.

Intermediaries: can both supply and demand types of social finance as well as facilitate relationships between other stakeholders and/or provide specific expertise in, for example, contracting.

Social finance institutions and mechanisms

Microfinance institutions (MFIs): offer a variety of financial products, such as microcredit loans for business or personal use, microsavings and microinsurance, and non-financial services (microfinance-plus), such as financial literacy training and access to health services, to individuals who cannot access mainstream financial institutions. MFIs are active across low-, middle- and high-income countries.

Credit co-operatives: offer financial products to its members who own and control the organisation. Credit unions are a well-known example.

Social banks: broadly relate to institutions offering banking and financial services to individuals, businesses and organisations with explicit social, environmental and/or sustainability goals. Often referred to as ethical, green or sustainable banks they include banks, such as Triodos Bank, as well as some forms of MFIs and credit unions.

Impact bonds: are a form of Payment-by-Results that seek to leverage capital from private, philanthropic and/or third-sector investors to fund social and public services. The two main forms are social impact bonds (SIBs) and development impact bonds (DIBs). The main difference between SIBs and DIBs is the outcome payer; a government agency or body only (SIB) and an external third party, such as an aid agency, philanthropic foundation or charity, alone or alongside the domestic government (DIB).

Venture philanthropy: investors utilise techniques associated with venture capital to offer financial and, sometimes, non-financial support to businesses and organisations aiming to have a social impact.

Crowdfunding: a form of peer-to-peer monetary financing for individuals, businesses or organisations through donations, rewards, debt or equity.

A (brief) history of social finance

It is widely recognised that the 2008 global financial crisis acted as a stimulus for social finance. New forms, such as impact bonds (see Chapter 5), were developed, and the term social finance came into popular usage as a way to collectively refer to the different individual forms of finance that are concerned with achieving social and/or environmental impact. However, using finance to generate social impact is not a new idea. Informal initiatives and more formal institutions and funds have existed for centuries to serve the needs of those worse off in society.

Versions of informal nonmarket initiatives, such as interfamily and friend relationships, savings clubs, rotating savings and credit associations (RoSCAs) and accumulating savings and credit associations (ASCAs), are a mainstay in societies throughout the world. Reciprocal interest-free loan arrangements, gifts and parties occur between family, friends and neighbours as (non-)monetary exchanges in communities within developing and more developed economies (14,15). Savings clubs run by a local community can act as a 'safe haven' where households or individuals store any excess money that is accessed on an agreed-upon date; for example, money for a Christmas Club might be accessed on the 1st of December (16). RoSCAs are widespread in communities throughout the world. They are referred to by different names in different countries, for example, *Pandero* in Peru, *Chit Funds* in India and *Pari* in Mali and a *ménage* or *menodge* in Scotland (14,17). In general, they refer to individuals from a local community regularly making monetary contributions to a fund that is distributed in rotation, wholly or in part, to each member of the fund (18). Finally, ASCAs are another type of financial self-help group. They differ from RoSCAs in a few ways. ASCAs accept more irregular and different-sized payments from members and members receive interest-bearing loans (19).

Alongside these informal initiatives are more formal institutions and funds with a social purpose. Tottenham Benefit Bank in London, Ruthwell Savings Bank in Scotland and the Bank for Savings in New York, established in 1804, 1810 and 1819 respectively, are early examples of savings banks that explicitly aimed to serve and aid poorer individuals in society (20). Irish loan funds were providing a form of microcredit to around 20% of Irish households in the mid-19th century (21). In Germany, rural Raiffeisen and urban Schulze-Delitzsch credit co-operatives were established in the 19th century to meet the needs of individuals with low incomes who previously had to rely on local moneylenders charging high-interest rates (20). Contemporary credit unions are a legacy of these credit co-operatives. See Box 2.2 for further detail of these initiatives and institutions.

A wide range of other initiatives also exist. The important point is that the origins of social finance, which is often considered a modern and innovative development, have roots in the work undertaken by informal community practices, faith-based and charitable models, funds, initiatives and institutions throughout the world (22).

Box 2.2   Formal institutions and funds with a social purpose

There are many early examples of savings banks and loan funds explicitly aimed at serving people with low incomes. Some notable ones written about in the literature are as follows:

Tottenham Benefit Bank (est. 1804)
Founded by Priscilla Wakefield, an author and Quaker, in London, and thought to be the first savings bank. Any sum of one shilling upwards could be deposited, and receive interest of 5%. (No longer exists.)

Ruthwell Savings Bank (est. 1810)
Established by Henry Duncan, a local parish minister in Southwest Scotland, sixpence was enough to open an account. Interest was paid at 5%, and surpluses went towards social projects, such as the establishment of a local school. Due to growth in other financial institutions, the final 29 accounts were transferred to Annan Savings Bank in 1875. The original building for the Bank now operates as a savings bank museum.

Airdrie Savings Bank (est. 1835)
Modelled on Ruthwell, the Airdrie Savings Bank is worth mentioning because it existed until 2017. At its peak, it had several branches throughout central Scotland.

Bank for Savings in the City of New York (est. 1819)
This was one of the first savings banks in the USA and initially promoted as a 'bank for the poor.' (Merged with Buffalo Savings Bank in 1982.)

Irish Loan Funds
Operating from around 1720, Irish Loan Funds were providing a form of microcredit to around 20% of Irish households in the mid-19th century and lasted until around 1915. Many had closed before then, due to economic pressures caused by the Great Famine (1845–1849) but also more restrictive regulations thought to have been introduced on the back of pressure from

---

major banks. Part of the reason these funds are so well-known is due to the records maintained by the Irish Reproductive Loan Fund – maintained at the National Archives in London – which has led to substantial amounts of research being conducted on them.

Rural Raiffeisen and urban Schulze-Delitzsch

Franz Hermann Schulze-Delitzsch was responsible for organising the world's first credit unions in Germany in 1850. These were co-operatives established to meet the needs of individuals with low incomes who previously had to rely on local moneylenders charging high-interest rates. Contemporary credit unions are a legacy of these credit co-operatives. These expanded rapidly in urban settings and later in rural locations, the latter often credited to Friedrich Wilhelm Raiffeisen. Raiffeisen was also associated with cooperative approaches to the procurement and distribution of food amongst the poorest in society. Through mergers and other developments, several forms of these innovations still exist in Germany today.

Rochdale Pioneers and Fenwick Weavers

UK versions of such cooperatives are the Rochdale Society of Equitable Pioneers (formed in 1844, and the forerunner of the UK cooperative movement) and, in Scotland, the Fenwick Weavers Society (established in 1761). The latter was initially concerned with ensuring standards in weaving but later expanded to bulk buying of goods and books, and even established a library (in 1808).

Grameen Bank and Muhammad Yunus

Of course, the most famous modern-day pioneer of socially purposeful microfinance, aimed at overcoming predatory lending, is Professor Muhammad Yunus, after whom our own research centre is named. Grameen Bank was originated by Yunus in 1976 and pioneered group lending. The Bank now has over nine million borrowers, over 90% of whom are women. Grameen has now expanded to several countries; most notably Grameen America now has 19 branches in 11 US cities. Grameen and Yunus were jointly awarded the Nobel Peace Prize in 2006. Microfinance was also, in part, the subject of the Nobel Prize in Economic Sciences, awarded to Abhijit Banerjee, Esther Duflo and Michael Kremer in 2019. It is unique for microfinance to have been the subject of Nobels in two fields.

Why is there a need for social finance?

Now that we have an idea of what social finance is, another important question is why is there a need for it? The main reasons relate to equity and social efficiency. Why are individuals, businesses and organisations unable to get the capital they need? Is this fair? Relatedly, but more of an efficiency argument, can we achieve positive economic and social outcomes from resources put into social finance initiatives? Answers to these questions, as well as being empirical (which we address in later chapters), lie in two key concepts; market failure and efficiency.

Market failure

Market failure occurs when there is not an efficient allocation of resources between providers and consumers. In the case of financial market failures, individuals, businesses or organisations (i.e. consumers) are either not able to gain access to formal financial providers or the types of finance provided are not suitable for their needs, when, with fuller information about risks, ability to pay or important social benefits, transactions could more-readily take place. The two main causes of such market failure are information asymmetries and externalities.

Information asymmetries

Information asymmetries exist when one party in a transaction has more or better information than the other (23,24). The uncertainty caused by this can lead to the cost and supply of goods set at a level that is not optimum in terms of efficiency (i.e. allocating resources in a way to generate the maximum societal benefits). Imagine a market with one consumer and one provider. The consumer has a maximum amount that they are willing to pay for a particular good and the provider a minimum they are willing to accept to cover the cost of producing the good. If both parties are fully informed, in theory, they will agree upon a price and quantity of the good that perfectly maximises their surplus. For a consumer this is the difference between their willingness to pay and the actual amount paid for the good, and for the producer the difference between the amount received for the good and the cost of producing the good. But rarely, if ever, is there perfect information. This manifests in two specific types of asymmetric information: adverse selection and moral hazard. We describe the implications of these forms of asymmetric information below using the specific case of a lender (i.e. the provider) and a borrower (i.e. the consumer) of a loan. For a more in-depth discussion of these issues see, for example, Stiglitz and Weiss (25); Stiglitz (26); Arnott and Stiglitz (27); Ghosh et al. (28).

ADVERSE SELECTION

Adverse selection is concerned with consumers' and providers' knowledge of risk; consumers generally having a better idea of their risk status. In the case of issuing a loan, the lender wants to identify whether a potential borrower is 'safe' or 'risky' in terms of their probability of making loan repayments. One strategy is for lenders to issue a single community interest rate, based on some perception of average default rates in a population and applicable to all potential borrowers with the intention of offsetting the risk of loan defaults. Lenders may do this if they have no idea about the riskiness of potential borrowers. However, if potential borrowers perceive themselves as low-risk, the standardised interest rate will likely be too high for them. They may then exit the borrower pool, which inadvertently increases the risk profile of, and associated interest rate for, the remaining applicants. Many may be willing to accept the higher rate, but, for others, the new higher rate will lead to a further round of exits, and so on. Alternatively, and using this revealed information, lenders may try to tailor their offerings more accurately to risk. In modern markets, lenders typically utilise an individual's credit score facilitated by credit bureaus for this purpose. Thus, a cycle is set in motion whereby lower-cost loans can be offered to lower-risk borrowers and the opposite for higher-risk borrowers. However, credit scores are imperfect and it is often a difficult, time-consuming and costly task to collect information by other means to assess the creditworthiness of potential clients. Of course, collateral can typically serve to reduce a lender's risk. However, some borrowers, particularly those with low incomes, lack collateral that would compensate lenders in the event of a loan default. If these lending mechanisms are not available to reduce the lender's risk, lenders may inadvertently reject 'safe' borrowers or choose to exit that particular market rather than lend to potentially high-risk borrowers. Such an outcome has social consequences.

A group of borrowers, most likely among those who are less well-off, are likely to be unfairly categorised as high-risk when they have the means to repay loans and loans are likely to be beneficial for them. This will leave them either financially excluded, without access to needed financial products to start or develop their own business or manage their financial lives, or forced to seek more expensive finance from non-responsible sub-prime lenders or local moneylenders with unfavourable repayment mechanisms. Given the well-documented links between, for example, these types of debt and health (see Chapter 6) this could have impacts beyond the financial that are negative. In short, a lender and a borrower who would otherwise enter into a transaction in a well-functioning market cannot do so, leaving the latter excluded from formal markets and perhaps even less-well-off (both financially and in terms of their well-being) from taking an informal loan. Furthermore, an often-overlooked aspect of market failure in this regard is that of externalities. Although explained in more detail below, a positive externality could also exist if other members of society not only care about these otherwise-excluded individuals gaining access to beneficial financial products but also being willing to pay to subsidise such access. Lenders may also lose out in this situation, as the exclusion of borrowers shrinks the size of the market available to them. To some degree, self-generated, market mechanisms can repair such informational asymmetries and lack of collateral through innovative lending mechanisms; see, for example, discussion of group lending by microcredit providers in Chapter 6. However, this approach may still suffer from significant degrees of market failure. The fixed costs of loan administration could add such a premium to the interest rate (of the sort that would not exist with larger providers and larger loans) that creditworthy people are once again excluded or leads to lenders altering their business model to target marginally better-off individuals with larger loans. In such a situation, the existence of positive externalities could justify public subsidisation of such administrative costs to circumvent these issues.

MORAL HAZARD

While adverse selection is concerned with the informational asymmetries before loan issuance, moral hazard focuses on what happens after loan issuance. In this situation, borrowers again hold an informational advantage over lenders. Two forms of moral hazard follow: ex-ante and ex-post.

Ex-ante moral hazard refers to lenders being unable to observe the actions of borrowers after loan issuance but before realising returns. As per adverse selection, one strategy open to lenders is to raise interest rates to generate a higher return as compensation for issuing what could be a risky loan. However, the knock-on effect of this is that borrowers face increased costs. Borrowers may then use their loan to fund projects with potentially higher returns but lower chances of success. As money is fungible even if the use is agreed with lenders in advance, borrowers are relatively unconstrained with how they use the loan once it is received. Another potential unintended consequence of high-interest rates is borrowers applying less effort to generate returns because of the opportunity cost associated with their labour. Again, lack of collateral amplifies this problem for lenders as they bear the costs of borrowers defaulting on loans.

Ex-post moral hazard, also known as the enforcement problem, is concerned with difficulties after loan use. Lenders may face two distinct problems. First, if lenders cannot observe the amount of profit made by a borrower; a borrower could feign default even when they realise a profit. Second, lenders may fully observe the profits made but cannot enforce repayment. Again, interest rates play a role as higher rates can increase the prospect of voluntary default. Consequently, if lenders cannot incentivise borrowers to make repayments, lenders may choose not to issue a loan.

The social consequences of moral hazard are the same as adverse selection. A segment of society, again most likely those who are less well-off and often more in need of a loan, will be excluded from the market and forced to seek another, potentially, non-optimal solution, while lenders will miss out on profits from not serving this group.

Externalities

In the example described above, there are only two parties in the financial transaction: the lender (i.e. the provider) and the borrower (i.e. the consumer). However, often transactions directly impact a third party; so those not directly involved in the transaction. This impact is called an externality and can be positive or negative.

Negative externalities are detrimental impacts on societal resources or well-being not accounted for in calculations of the costs of production or benefits from consumption. If accounted for, less of the goods concerned might be produced or consumed. This is the opposite of positive externalities; whereby accounting for social benefits might lead to more of the good concerned being produced and provided. Everyday examples include air pollution from factories (negative externalities) and reducing deforestation (positive externalities). When the market fails to adequately incorporate these externalities, the price mechanism alone is not sufficient to efficiently allocate resources for maximisation of social benefits (1,4). Some sort of regulation or alternative form of provision is required.

Why is the failure to incorporate externalities important? Typically, the market is only concerned with financial returns. This corresponds to Milton Friedman's (29, p. 17) famous credo that "there is one and only one social responsibility of business – to use its resources and engage in activities designed to increase its profits ... ." However, failure to account appropriately for externalities can mean the real benefit or cost of a transaction is not reflected in the price or financial return. It is this failure that results in an allocation of resources that does not maximise the overall benefit to society as transactions occur which should not and others do not happen which should. We can see examples of externalities from the social consequences of market failure resulting from information asymmetries between a lender (i.e. the provider) and borrower (i.e. the consumer) of a loan.

As outlined above, a segment of society, who are less well-off and in need of a loan, will be excluded from the market because of information asymmetries. This generates positive and negative externalities. A specific positive externality is the 'caring externality.' This was first articulated in relation to the provision of healthcare in the UK through the NHS (30,31). The reason why the NHS, funded directly through taxation, is accepted is that "individuals are affected by others' health status for the simple reason that most of them care" (30, p. 89); this is discussed more fully in relation to healthcare in Chapter 3. A similar argument is possible for the provision of financial products to the financially excluded – a market failure exists because other members of society care about these individuals gaining access to beneficial financial products and services and would be willing to affect such access by sacrificing some of their own resources – most efficiently achieved through the taxation framework. Financial exclusion leading to negative externalities also enhances this case. Financially excluded individuals can turn to family and friends, informal moneylenders and/or different forms of subprime lenders for loans. If seeking a financial safety net from friends and family becomes commonplace this could place a strain on these relationships, transforming them from a social to a financial relationship with negative consequences. Using informal moneylenders and/or forms of subprime lenders who do not have the interests of borrowers as their primary concern increases the risk of these individuals getting into unmanageable debt as profit drives lenders' decisions. For example, lenders may offer loans when this could make borrowers' situation worse i.e. when they already have multiple loans from other lenders and are struggling to make repayments. This will not only impact negatively on the individual in question but also the lives of close family and/or friends and/or the state who have to intervene with well-being and/or financial support. For both types of externality, extending the provision of financial products in a responsible way could ensure the capture of social benefits (i.e. positive externalities) and minimisation of social costs (i.e. negative externalities). Again, this is likely to require government intervention to spend the wider population's tax dollars on subsidising those responsible lenders that target the worst-off creditworthy individuals and provide (non-revenue-earning) advice.

Efficiency

Efficiency refers to using resources in a way that maximises benefits and minimises costs. Of key concern is the idea of opportunity costs. Resources used in one way cannot be used in another; the benefits forgone are the opportunity costs. This is of particular importance in the context of fixed government budgets. In this situation, resources are scarce – we cannot fund everything we want and this necessitates hard choices between competing claims on resources (i.e. trade-offs). If resources are inefficiently used, reallocation could increase social benefits. These economic principles have permeated government decision-making, particularly as governments' role in society changed during the 20th century.

Following the Second World War, governments in the majority of high-income countries assumed the role of providing social and public services. However, from the 1970s the role of government has been changing in these countries following the emergence and now dominance of the market economy. This has seen a shift in how government operates from a high, centralised tax and spend model with nationalised public services towards a lower taxation approach and a focus on privatisation. This process was supercharged following the 2008 financial crisis that resulted in a period of prolonged and self-enforced austerity, which only eased due to pressures from the COVID-19 pandemic. Alongside this change in ideological approach to government was public service reform. New Public Management (NPM) is described as having "swept through the Anglosphere in the late 1980s and 1990s" (32, p. 2). NPM is associated with embedding aspects of the market in public sector delivery, such as increased competition, a more explicit focus on performance management and efficient resource use (see Hood (33) for an in-depth overview of NPM). This resulted in government's role shifting towards one of commissioning rather than delivering public and social services (1). These ideological approaches in addition to, and alongside issues of, market failure helped create the conditions for social finance to emerge.

The emergence of social finance

Social finance represents a new way of doing finance that responds to market failures and government's concern for efficiency. These reasons apply to a greater and lesser extent with different forms of social finance. An exemplar of the latter is impact bonds and the former is microcredit.

A primary goal of impact bonds is to use scarce public funding more efficiently. By building on the Payment-by-Results model, investors, who front the capital for interventions, only receive payment from the outcome payer, typically government, upon meeting agreed outcomes. Impact bonds are viewed as extending the focus of NPM from alternative service delivery to alternative service funding with service providers paid for meeting outcomes (34,35); recent evidence also suggests impact bonds entrench values associated with NPM in public service reform (32). See Chapter 5 for an in-depth discussion of impact bonds.

Microfinance institutions are well-known for having a double-bottom line concerned with financial and social impact. In fact, the advent of green microfinance has brought environmental concerns to the fore and introduced the idea of a triple-bottom-line. This means that social and environmental impacts are generally an explicit concern and externalities are brought into the decision-making process. This leads to different decisions about who is eligible to receive a loan and the market served. To overcome market failures caused by information asymmetries, these institutions have developed innovative lending and repayment mechanisms, such as joint-liability, group and progressive lending, and more frequent repayment schedules. While microfinance institutions are predominantly associated with low- and middle-income countries, variants also operate in high-income countries of, for example, Europe and North America where they are more likely to target individuals at the lower end of the market as opposed to other social finance providers, such as credit unions, which generally target relatively more-affluent households. This provision of microcredit, in responding to market failures, also laid the groundwork for other forms of microfinance, such as microsavings and microinsurance, and microfinance-plus (see Chapters 6 and 7 for further discussion).

Conclusion

In setting out in broad terms what social finance is, where it emerged from and why it is needed we provide the basis from which to move into new territory: exploration of the role of different forms of social finance – impact bonds and microfinance – in responding to specific global health challenges. Namely, the *funding* of health and health(care) services (impact bonds), *access* to these same services (microfinance products and microfinance-plus) and *acting on* other pathways to health (microcredit and impact bonds) (see Chapters 5, 6, 7). While this is an under-recognised and under-developed area, it stems from recognising the social as well as economic benefits of social finance and the areas of market failures and efficiency that social finance specifically targets. Before evidencing what we know about social finance acting in this way, the next two chapters will provide the conceptual links between social finance and these challenges to open up the 'evaluative space' of this new area of social finance and health.

References

1. Nicholls A, Emerson J. Social Finance: Capitalizing Social Impact. In: *Social Finance*. Oxford University Press; 2015.
2. Salway M, Palmer P, Clifford J. *Demystifying Social Finance and Social Investment*. Routledge; 2020.
3. Nicholls A. The institutionalization of social investment: The interplay of investment logics and investor rationalities.*Journal of Social Entrepreneurship*. 2010;1(1):70–100.

4. Andrikopoulos A. *The Essentials of Social Finance*. Routledge; 2021.

5. Nicholls A, Pharoah C. *The Landscape of Social Investment: A Holistic Topology of Opportunities and Challenges*. Oxford: Skoll Centre for Social Entrepreneurship; 2007.

6. Fuller D, Jonas A. Alternative Financial Spaces. In: *Alternative Economic Spaces*. London: SAGE Pubications; 2003. p. 55–74.

7. Jonas AEG. Interrogating Alternative Local and Regional Economies: The British Credit Union Movement and Post-Binary Thinking. In: *Alternative Economies and Spaces: New Perspectives for a Sustainable Economy*. Bielefeld: Verlag; 2013. pp. 23–43.

8. McHugh N, Baker R, Donaldson C. Microcredit for enterprise in the UK as an 'alternative' economic space. *Geoforum*. 2019;100:80–88.

9. Research and Markets. Microfinance – Global Market Trajectory & Analytics. 2022.

10. Gustafsson-Wright E, Bogglid-Jones I, Nwabunnia O, Osborne S. *Social and Development Impact Bonds by the Numbers*. February 2022 snapshot. Brookings Institution; 2022. (Global Impact Bond Database).

11. GIIN. Annual Impact Investor Survey 2020. The Tenth Edition. 2020.

12. IFC. Growing Impact. *New Insights into the Practice of Impact Investing*. International Finance Corporation; 2020.

13. GSIA. *Global Sustainable Investment Review 2012*. Washington DC: Global Sustainable Investment Alliance; 2013.

14. Biosca O, McHugh N, Ibrahim F, Baker R, Laxton T, Donaldson C. Walking a tightrope: Using financial diaries to investigate day-to-day financial decisions and the social safety net of the financially excluded. *The ANNALS of the American Academy of Political and Social Science*. 2020; 689(1):46–64.

15. Rutherford S. Money talks: Conversations with poor households in Bangladesh about managing money. *Journal of Microfinance*. 2004;5(2): 43–75.

16. Thaler RH, Shefrin HM. An economic theory of self-control. *Journal of Political Economy*. 1981;2(89):392–406.

17. Bouman FJA. ROSCA: On the origin of species. *Savings and Development*. 1995;2(19):117–146.

18. Ardener S. The comparative study of rotating credit associations. *Journal of Anthropological Institute of Great Britain and Ireland*. 1964;2(94):201–229.

19. Bouman FJA. Rotating and accumulating savings and credit associations: A development perspective. *World Development*. 1995;23(3):371–384.

20. Vittas D. *Thrift Deposit Institutions in EUrope and the United States*. The World Bank; 1995.

21. Hollis A, Sweetman A. Microcredit: What can we learn from the past? *World Development*. 1998;26(10):1875–1891.

22. Mulgan G. Social Finance: Does "Investment" Add Value? In: *Social Finance*. Routledge; 2015. p. 45–63.

23. Akerlof G. The market for "Lemons": Quality uncertainty and the market mechanism. *Quarterly Journal of Economics*. 1970;84(3):488–500.

24. Ross SA. The economic theory of agency: The principal's problem. *The American Economic Review*. 1973;2(3):134–139.

25. Stiglitz JE, Weiss A. Credit Rationing in Markets with Imperfect Information. 1981;3(71):393–410.
26. Stiglitz JE. Peer monitoring and credit markets. *The World Bank Economic Review*. 1990;3(4):351–366.
27. Arnott R, Stiglitz JE. Moral hazard and nonmarket institutions: Dysfunctional crowding out of peer monitoring? *The American Economic Review*. 1991;81: 179–190.
28. Ghosh P, Mookherjee D, Ray D. Credit Rationing in Developing Countries: 1999;24.
29. Friedman M. *A Friedman doctrine-- The Social Responsibility Of Business Is to Increase Its Profits*. The New York Times; 1970.
30. Culyer AJ. *Need and the National Health Service: Economics and Social Choice*. Oxford: Martin Robertson; 1976.
31. Culyer AJ. The nature of the commodity healthcare and its efficient allocation. *Oxford Economic Papers*. 1971;23:189–211.
32. French M, Kimmitt J, Wilson R, Jamieson D, Lowe T. Social impact bonds and public service reform: Back to the future of new public management? *International Public Management Journal*. 2022;21.
33. Hood C. A public management for all seasons? *Public Administration*. 1991; 69(1):3–19.
34. Joy M, Shields J. Social impact bonds: The next phase of third sector marketization? *Canadian Journal of Nonprofit and Social Economy Research*. 2013;4(2):39–55.
35. Warner ME. Private finance for public goods: Social impact bonds. *Journal of Economic Policy Reform*. 2013;16(4):303–319.

3 Rethinking ... the funding of healthcare

Introduction

Healthcare in almost all advanced economies is publicly funded. In the United Kingdom (UK), at the time of writing, for example, the National Health Service (NHS) is approaching its 75th birthday. However, there is now a global initiative – known as Universal Health Coverage (UHC) – to move all countries towards this. How different countries achieve this, at what pace and what they include in the funding package will be different. On this last issue, it is worth noting at the outset that, in many countries, services aimed at improving public (or population) health are often defined as within the package. More relevant to this volume, even those countries with more established publicly funded systems often still struggle to fully meet the needs of their populations and, thus, may look to innovate, amongst other things, with respect to funding sources. In each case, of seeking UHC or reforming more established publicly funded systems, there is a potential role for social finance.

In this chapter, we seek to explain why it is that governments are involved in healthcare financing, even in insurance-based systems such as the United States of America (USA). Although there are strong moral and political cases for government intervention in healthcare, we will focus here on the economic case, which stems from notions of market failure. We then address the issues of how such funding mechanisms are challenged and what might be a potential role for social finance – in the form of healthcare funded through microfinance and impact bonds. (Note each may also have a role in addressing wider – social – determinants of health as addressed later, initially in Chapter 4.)

Why do we care? Or, why do governments 'interfere' in healthcare?

Across the globe, healthcare funding is dominated by public sources of finance, be it through taxation or social insurance. The most-established

DOI: 10.4324/9781003305248-5

economies are in this situation already, whilst most other countries are seeking to move in this direction. If UHC is to be achieved, it is hard to envisage this coming about without significant government intervention. This dominance of public funding in healthcare lies as much in economic as well as humanitarian arguments. The economic arguments are not financial either, but rather rest on three sources of market failure, first brought together by Canadian economist, Robert Evans (1). In economics, market failure does not equate to a dislike of free markets. Many of us dislike the fact that only some people can afford luxury cars, but rarely do we hear a case being made for a National Car Service. Market failure is quite specific, arising when markets struggle to account fully for important characteristics of commodities; rendering their allocation sub-optimal relative to when governments intervene. A NHS, as in the UK, is an extreme, but justifiable and popular, form of this. But what is the market failure case?

Private sources of financing

Without government intervention, insurance markets would develop to deal with unpredictable healthcare needs. The basic principle is quite straightforward. Through payment of a relatively small fee (commonly known as a premium), an individual or family is protected against the financial risk associated with care requirements should they contract an illness requiring significant amounts of (costly) care. Such insurance markets are commonplace throughout the world. They take different forms, of course. Generally, the size of the premium is tailored to risk. Consumers can mitigate the premium size by paying user charges (sometimes known as co-insurance or deductibles, and usually up to a specified limit beyond which insurance covers the full costs of care).

Of course, where insurance markets are not well developed, consumers would be liable for the full cost of care in the form of out-of-pocket payments, which would be highly prohibitive for many, especially in lower-income countries.

The failure of private insurance

With financial risks mitigated by insurance, 'moral hazard' arises. This is a classic problem in insurance markets whereby, with a third party (the insurance company) paying the bills, costs receive less emphasis in decisions of consumers and providers. Such moral hazard is behind historic healthcare cost inflation in the USA, as witnessed by USA spending far outstripping that of any other country listed in Table 3.1. This is exacerbated by administrative costs (of billing and advertising) which inflate premiums so much that people who would otherwise be

Table 3.1 Total health expenditure, and percentage of total that is public, in OECD countries (1990 and 2019)

Country	1990 total health exp US$PPP	% public	2019 total health exp US$PPP	% public	Absolute % increase
Australia	1318	67	4919	69	+2
Austria	1205	74	5705	75	+1
Canada	1678	75	5370	70	−5
Czech Rep	576	96	3417	82	−14
Denmark	1453	83	5478	83	=
Finland	1292	81	4561	80	−1
France	1520	78	5274	77	−1
Germany	1602	76	6518	78	+2
Greece	707	63	2319	60	−3
Iceland	1376	87	4541	83	−4
Ireland	796	72	5083	75	+3
Italy	1321	78	3653	74	−4
Japan	1082	78	4691	84	+6
South Korea	371	37	3406	60	+23
Luxembourg	1486	93	5414	86	−7
Mexico	260	41	1133	50	+9
Netherlands	1403	78	5739	76	−2
N Zealand	937	82	4212	79	−3
Norway	1363	83	6745	86	+3
Poland	258	96	2289	71	−25
Portugal	614	65	3347	61	−4
Spain	815	79	3600	70	−9
Sweden	1492	90	5552	85	−5
Switzerland	1782	68	7138	32	−36
Turkey	171	61	1267	78	+17
UK	968	84	4500	79	−5
USA	2738	40	10,948	51	+11

Source: OECD (2). Public funding is calculated using spending by government schemes and social health insurance.

$PPP (Purchasing Power Parity) is simply a form of currency conversion making spends across countries more easily comparable.

insured are priced out of the market. Organisation for Economic Co-operation and Development (OECD) data for 2018 show that administrative costs account for 9% of total costs in the USA compared with 3% in Canada and approximately 2% in the UK (2).

In public systems, government funding and supply-side controls (limiting human and capital resource) make it easier to control costs and spread administrative burdens across large populations. A naïve observer would promote user charges to control costs. However, charges simply encourage the system to switch its caregiving powers to those willing and able to pay. Exemptions help, but add further administration costs. These challenges are eliminated with extensive government intervention.

Lack of consumer knowledge

Markets work well in maintaining quality when consumers are informed, which is less so in healthcare. For example, it may be thought more of a fundamental human right for people to have access to food than healthcare. Yet, for food, beyond some income supplementation for those on lower incomes, there is little interference in the demand side of the market; consumers being left to make their own judgements. This is largely because most people know what they like, or at least this is assumed to be the case. The consequences of mistakes are not great either. Safety and quality are handled via systems of standards and regulation on the supply side, beyond which retailers compete for custom. However, in healthcare, due to the lack of knowledge amongst 'consumers' as to the technical relationship between care and its possible outcomes, to maintain standards, we grant licenses to qualified professionals to advise us and, occasionally, even make decisions on our behalf. Although the right thing to do, this conflation of demand and supply inadvertently creates powerful professional bodies, such as the medical profession, requiring 'countervailing power' of government to negotiate over important issues such as pay and provision. Without this, providers could use their knowledge advantage to specify care packages that may not be in line with what a fully informed consumer would wish; thus, requiring government, with its countervailing collective power, to step in.

The 'caring externality': Markets don't care, but people do

Well-functioning insurance markets tailor premiums to risk. However, this leads the rich (usually healthier) to pay less while those in greater need (usually on lower incomes) pay more. For example, imagine a single insurer, with little advanced knowledge of individual risks in a community. The insurer might initially arrive at a premium based on the average risk across the community; a 'community rate.' This will cause many in healthier (and usually also wealthier) groups to remove themselves from the market, as they would perceive the premium to be too high relative to their own personal risk level. The insurer might see this and tailor premiums at a lower level to this group. But this would then leave the average risk level, and consequent premium for the remainder of the main group, to now be higher than when all were included in the original community rating. This will cause the next healthiest group to perceive the new premium as too high and so on. Thus, a vicious cycle of 'adverse selection' is set off, the market segments, and different types of premium and likely levels of care quality are offered to different groups, further exacerbating inequalities. Although, in a sense, adverse selection is an example of the market actually functioning well (in identifying risk levels and tailoring premiums appropriately), it also counts as market failure, as those most vulnerable (i.e. at higher risk of being ill) are more likely not to be able to afford such tailor-made premiums or to access care in such a market. In many societies, this is something that we care about, with the better off (or those with access) willing to contribute to access for others; but often within the one unified system as opposed to having a charitable arm with lower-quality care. Markets, focusing only on individuals acting on their own behalf, cannot facilitate this. The most effective way to achieve the transfers necessary to ensure universal coverage is through some form of public financing, such as taxation.

Implications of market failure

Despite differences across countries, the stunning common feature, internationally, is achievement of (or moves towards) universal coverage through collective, not private, 'insurance.' This is illustrated in Table 3.1. Over a 30-year period, ending just prior to the COVID-19 pandemic, a high proportion of healthcare spending coming from the public purse has been maintained. In 10 of the 27 countries listed in Table 3.1, this proportion has even increased over this period. The facts are that government intervention in healthcare is a global phenomenon. This is a key point to take account of in many contexts in which social finance initiatives are being considered.

With insurance based on groups, attempts are made to work out entitlements for everyone, which obviously creates tensions as there are only limited resources available in total. A different kind of 'contract' is created between patients and payers in a public as opposed to a private system. Generally, people have to wait longer in publicly funded systems because bed occupancy rates tend to be higher; peak flows of demands on the system are harder to accommodate when, on average throughout the year, 90% of beds are occupied. In the USA, only about two-thirds of beds are occupied on average; this is because, when one is paying privately, as is the case for around 50% of USA healthcare expenditures, the 'contract' requires instant access to care once a diagnosis is made. Thus more 'spare capacity' is required of a private system to ensure peak flows of demand combined with instant access can be met. Another key aspect associated with publicly funded healthcare, however, ensures that standards are maintained in such a constrained environment. This is the characteristic of compulsion, whereby, with the vocal middle classes locked in, the demands they might place on the system in terms of maintenance of quality end up being of benefit to those who are more vulnerable and less able to advocate for themselves. Otherwise, such latter groups would get left behind in terms of standards of service offered if the middle classes were able to opt-out completely – the classic 'two-tier system' would emerge.

The above arguments present a strong, many would say compelling, case for significant government intervention in healthcare, but does not prescribe exactly what form such intervention should take. Thus, although most advanced economies of the world seem to have adopted publicly funded systems, the details of these systems vary greatly. Generally, however, two main types of public funding exist, as listed in Table 3.2. Through the element of compulsion mentioned above, everyone except those in some vulnerable groups or who are retired has to pay their taxes or, to different degrees in Bismarkian-type systems, contribute to a sickness fund. Other systems might bear a resemblance to the Bismarkian model, but without necessarily recognising this and may embody important differences too.

Nevertheless, governments consistently complain about reduced abilities to invest in public services. A basic reason for this, including in the USA, is that such systems all face the same fundamental problem; once prices at the point of consumption of healthcare are covered

Table 3.2 Main types of publicly funded healthcare systems

System	General description of source of funds and objectives
Beveridge	• Established in UK after Second World War, arising from Beveridge Report first published in 1942, and is basis for UK and other systems now. • Funded from central or regional taxation. • Aimed at covering all inhabitants from outset. • If taxes are progressive (whereby) higher earners pay a higher percentage of extra income earned to government, then this system can be highly redistributive (i.e. transferring resources from rich to poor as well as healthy to unhealthy).
Bismarck	• Often termed 'social insurance' and established in Germany in late 19th Century (under Chancellor Bismarck), although much developed since then it is still the basis for the system in Germany (and other countries) now. • Funded from contributions from employees/employers, but now with state subsidies. • Initially aimed at providing a level of cover for payers. • Culturally, does not have same explicit redistributive agenda as Beveridge-type systems, although older people and unemployed are covered by other sources of funding, such as state subsidies.
Compulsory insurance	• Similar to social insurance, but based in countries where private insurance markets are a more established part of the infrastructure. • Insurance is mandated, with risk compensation schemes put in place by government to protect insurers from high-risk groups. • Some countries may require contributions to general taxation in order to facilitate compensation for the less-well-off.

(or heavily subsidised) by the state, claims on resources will be greater than the total resource available. Scarcity needs to be managed, leading to a set of common policy questions across such systems. For example, can user charges still be employed to moderate such claims and pressures on the system? Can market forces still be used within a publicly funded system, where healthcare providers compete for public funds? If there are limitations to charges and internal markets, what then? With governments spending public money in new and unexpected ways, shoring up the banks and other parts of the private sector, in addition to ever-increasing pressures of ageing societies and the growth of non-communicable diseases, can new forms of funding be found for public services?

Addressing these questions forms the journey of the book after Chapter 4. In seeking new forms of funding, a gradual privatisation of healthcare has been taking place in some major economies of the world already. Despite what we have said above, it cannot be denied that, in Table 3.1, there are some countries within which, despite being high, the proportion of healthcare spending coming from the public purse has decreased over the past 30 years. The opportunity is now here for more radical change in terms of alternative sources of financing, changing how public funds are utilised as well as adding to the traditional private sources of financing in the form of private insurance or through charges at the point of service delivery.

Data on lower-to-middle-income countries, although over a shorter period, shows a similar trend (3). World Bank data on 54 such countries shows that, on average, from 2011 to 2018, the percentage of Gross Domestic Product spent on healthcare rose from 2.8% to 4.1%. Although accompanied by shares of public and out-of-pocket sources, which are rising and falling respectively, progress has been slow. The share of health expenditures in such countries, which comes from the public purse is currently around 37%, which, again, creates potential for sources of social financing to act as alternatives to charges and private insurance.

Whither social financing?

One of the great ironies of healthcare financing is that, despite the strong equity-based arguments against user charges, they are highly prevalent in the lower-income countries of the world. As economies develop and decision-makers eventually begin to think about funding a more coherent healthcare system, the main challenge is found to be in having the state infrastructure in place to collect funds. Many lower-income countries lack a formal economy in the way that would be recognised in many higher-income countries, which makes collection of funds (in the form of taxes) difficult (4). Such countries, therefore, tend to start by

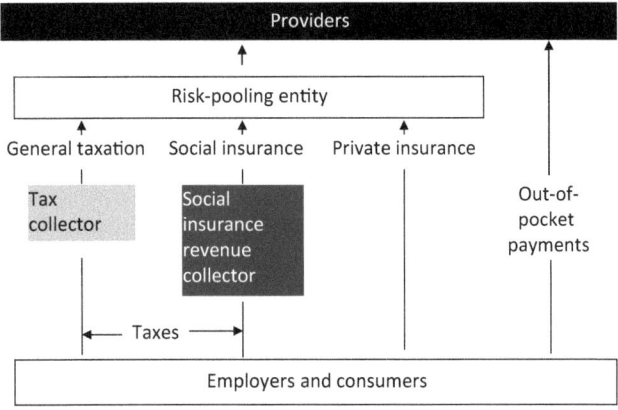

Figure 3.1 Types of healthcare financing.

taxing groups that are easy to capture, such as civil servants and other public sector employees, with the remainder of the population facing either severely limited access or paying privately.

This is illustrated, at least in part, by Figure 3.1, adapted from the work of Normand and Busse (5). The basic task of whatever healthcare system is in place is to get funds from employers and consumers into the hands of the providers (healthcare facilities and professionals) who provide care. As economies and infrastructure develop, and in line with the pursuit of UHC, the aim of most health policymakers becomes that of moving from the right side of Figure 3.1 towards the left where more and more payments are made into a collective fund, which could be private but is more often public.

However, whilst this is happening, and given the slow progress re-ferred to above, what are the masses of the least-well-off in the world to do in the meantime? Over the past 20–30 years, microfinancing has grown to provide basic packages of health services, funded by poor people paying small sums to a collective, sometimes with some subsidies and often run as a social business (i.e. where surpluses are reinvested into services and payments graded by income – with those who are better off paying in more) (6) (see Chapter 7 for a more in-depth discussion). This both mimics and is a hybrid of what we in the West might think of as the role of government along with insurance. We now know that, from the recent work of people like Dowla and Barua (7), the poorest people, even in global terms, will pay into such institutions. In Figure 3.2, this is characterised by shifting people from exposure to out-of-pocket pay-ments to a form of private (micro) insurance and, thus, risk-pooling;

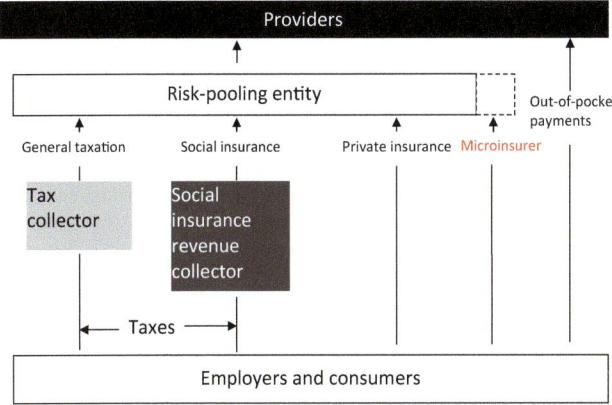

Figure 3.2 Influence of microfinance on types of healthcare financing.

although out-of-pocket financing can occur within private and more-public forms of insurance. Whether this is a case of markets adapting or reparation of a form of market failure is not clear, but it would certainly seem to be the case that microfinancing has, in part, filled a gap that governments and large financial institutions either could or would not and will need to be accounted for in policy as governments worldwide attempt to move towards UHC. An excellent example of high-tech success in this area, whereby small contributions even allow for cross-subsidisation, and thus enhanced access for those who are worst-off in terms of income, is provided by the Grameen Green Children Eye Hospital in Bogura, rural Bangladesh (see Box 3.1). A further, and important aspect of this, but one which is more difficult to represent in the Figure 3.2, is that microfinance initiatives, through their capturing of enrolees in less-well-off groups, often have health initiatives 'piggy-backed' onto them – commonly known as microfinance-plus.

The situation with impact bonds is less clear-cut. In Figure 3.3 we attempt to characterise the place of both social impact bonds (SIBs) and development impact bonds (DIBs) in healthcare financing. There is one initial point to note here. That is, our initial framework (in Figure 3.1) does not account for the role of foundations and charities in healthcare funding, especially the more significant role they are likely to have in lower- and middle-income countries. This is characterised by the addition of the 'Foundations, charities, etc.' to the box at the base of Figure 3.3. Normally, as with consumers and employers, such foundations and charities are trying to get resources (or financing) to providers. Importantly, such organisations may be outcome payers in the event of

---

Box 3.1 Grameen Green Children (GC) Eye Hospital in Bangladesh: a case study of microfinance and health (8,9)

Established in 2007, the Grameen GC Eye Hospital in Bogura, in rural Bangladesh, has become well known for the efficiency of its care processes as well as its financial sustainability. As part of Grameen Healthcare, its financing is based on the similar principles of social business as the better-known microfinance institution, Grameen Bank, originated by Nobel Peace Laureate, Muhammad Yunus. It also operates services at satellite camps in more remote areas.

Specialising in few eye treatments (such as cataract removal and repair) patients are given an eye test in order to 'screen' them into further testing and appropriate treatments. Multiple surgeons work simultaneously in the operating theatre in which some procedures can take as little as six minutes to complete, allowing for completion of 30–40 eye operations per day. Outcomes are good. Eighty-eight per cent of post-op patients have good vision, 7% higher than World Health Organization average.

The hospital is stocked with the best equipment from around the world and the clinicians have pioneered new approaches to tackling healthcare issues that hold back millions of people worldwide. Grameen delivers high-quality care at an affordable cost in high volume. It has highly trained technicians doing most of the examination and preparation work so that the ophthalmologists can focus on the operations.

The hospital is run on a cost-subsidy basis. There is a registration fee of $1.18, with outpatient visits costing the same. Depending on income and type of surgery, cataract surgery can range in price from approximately $60 to $880, with those who can afford it subsidising those who cannot. Ten per cent are treated free. For camp patients, most services are free with cataract surgery priced at around $30. To decide who should pay, and how much, a simple questionnaire is used. Of the 55,516 cataract surgeries performed since its inception to October 2022, 5,915 were provided for free to the poorest.

---

impact bonds, with which they are associated, meeting specified targets or, more likely, be investors in impact bonds providing the upfront capital and receiving outcome payments when targets are met. The basics of the latter type of such bonds are that a third-party investor would

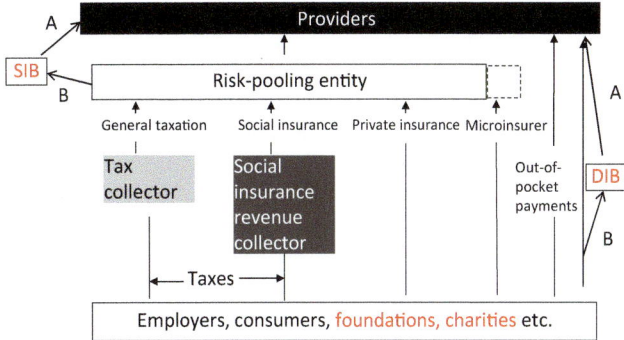

Figure 3.3 The place of impact bonds in healthcare financing.

put up some funds for the operation of services, with funds flowing, via an intermediary, to (existing or new) providers as in route A in Figure 3.3, for both SIBs, in the case of more-established publicly funded systems to left of Figure 3.3, and DIBs, in the case of foundations and charities to the right. The investment would have some targets associated with it in the form of health and well-being goals or those for accessing particular types of care. In the event of such targets being met, a payment would be triggered (e.g. from the public funder, respective foundation or charity). In Figure 3.3, this payment is signified by route B for each of SIBs or DIBs. In each case, it could be argued that all that is happening is that this payment of B occurs later than A.

Thus, although it seems that the investor is allowed to make a return on their initial outlay, based on achievement of health and healthcare goals, what is not clear is whether this draws more resources into healthcare systems, as, ultimately, the main payer for care will have to reimburse the investor, although this payment may be in conjunction with some other outcome payer(s). That main payer will likely be budget-constrained and, so, is merely paying for services in the way that they normally would. This would seem to be the case with respect to SIBs. However, for DIBs this is less clear. It may be that, through partnership arrangements, DIBs manage to draw more resources into healthcare systems and could even be seen as part of the desired transition from right to left in the above Figures. It may also be claimed impact bonds encourage speeding up of new service developments and also greater innovation in such development. Each of these claims would, of course, be open to question and subject to evidence from evaluatory studies. By definition, impact bonds are supposed to result in a transference of risk from public to private sectors. If the targets are not reached, the public funder (or other external third-party outcome payers in the case of DIBs) does not have to pay, although, of course, this may discourage future bond initiatives and also reduce targeting of such bonds at groups who may be in most need because they face particularly challenging barriers to change. An example of a social impact bond in a high-income country is given in Box 3.2. With respect to lower- and middle-income countries, the issues are the same, but, as stated above, it may be that the issuance of impact bonds by foundations, which are more prevalent in such countries, brings more resources into the system. When targets are reached, payments from the limited budgets of respective foundations would be triggered and, thus, still have to be made. Whether there are net gains, especially to service recipients and the wider public, from all of these complications is best informed by the evidence.

Box 3.2   Newcastle's 'Ways to Wellness': funded via a social impact bond (SIB)

'Ways to Wellness' is a community-based social prescribing initiative which involves identifying health well-being goals of participants and, consequently, increasing access to community and voluntary groups. Ways to Wellness comprises a 'hub' model of working in which a non-medical link worker, trained in behaviour change methods, offers a holistic and personalised service to identify meaningful health and wellness goals, as well as connecting clients, when indicated, to community and voluntary groups and resources.

Launched in 2015 as the UK's first health sector SIB, Ways to Wellness is funded up-front by Cabinet Office Social Outcomes Fund and the Newcastle West Clinical Commissioning Group (CCG). The CCG covers 17 General Practices located in one of the most socially-deprived areas of the UK. The intermediary is Bridges Fund Management. Paying 1.38 times the initial investment (of £1.65m) if targets are met over the first seven years (with a maximum outlay of £8.2m), this SIB aims to improve outcomes for 8,500 patients, aged 40–74 on registers of general practitioners and with Long-Term Conditions (LTCs), over its first seven years. LTCs included are diabetes (types 1 and 2), chronic obstructive pulmonary disease, asthma, chronic heart disease, epilepsy and osteoporosis. The two outcomes are improved self-management of LTCs leading to better well-being and reduced costs of secondary healthcare services. Early results show the programme working as expected in terms of patient recruitment and types of intervention co-produced by the link worker and patients (10).

Conclusion

The arguments above would rule out the market as a basis for financing whole healthcare systems. This also reflects international attempts to move towards UHC. However, this does not rule out the use of innovations based on market forces being used *within* such systems. Given the pressures placed on healthcare budgets, even in higher-income settings, it is not surprising, therefore, that governments will seek to experiment with such instruments. One such instrument is that of impact bonds. Likewise, where parts of society feel 'left behind' it is equally unsurprising that they take action into their own hands in the form of building insurance on top of microfinance initiatives.

The key questions, to be addressed in the remainder of the book, then become about the extent to which such initiatives are taken up or can grow, whether they match claims made with respect to innovation and meeting stated objectives or targets, and their implications for flows of funds into service provision and whether this adds to or detracts from the effectiveness, efficiency and equity of healthcare.

References

1. Evans R. *Strained Mercy: The Economics of Canadian Healthcare*. Toronto: Butterworth; 1984.
2. OECD. Health expenditure and financing. 2022.
3. World Bank. Current health expenditure (% of GDP) - Lower middle income. 2022.
4. Bachas P, Kondylis F, Loeser J. Increasing tax revenue in developing countries. *World Bank Blogs*. 2021.
5. Normand C, Busse R. Social health insurance financing. In: *Funding Healthcare: Options for Europe*. Buckingham (PA): Open University Press; 2000. p. 59–79.
6. Leatherman S, Geissler K, Gray B, Gash M. Health financing: A new role for microfinance institutions? *Journal of International Development*. 2013; 25(7):881–896.
7. Dowla A, Barua D. *The Poor Always Pay Back: The Grameen II Story*. Bloomfield CT: Kumarian Press; 2006.
8. Conniff S. What the NHS could learn from the Grameen Eye Hospital. *The Guardian*. 2010.
9. Grameen Healthcare Services Ltd. Grameen GC Eye Hospital-01, Bogura. 2022.
10. Moffatt S, Steer M, Lawson S, Penn L, O'Brien N. Link Worker social prescribing to improve health and well-being for people with long-term conditions: Qualitative study of service user perceptions. *BMJ Open*. 2017; 7(7):e015203.

4 Rethinking ... how to act on health inequalities

Introduction

In this chapter, we consider a much more pervasive role for social finance; beyond funding of healthcare and health services. Here, social finance is conceptualised as a stimulant to the determinants of health and, thus, as an enabler for reducing health inequalities. This potential is particularly important as the need for other non-healthcare (in the UK, non-National Health Service) means of acting on health has long been recognised (1,2). However, even in advanced economies of the world, health inequalities persist and, in some jurisdictions, are even widening. Hence, the need to think of new initiatives, such as social finance, acting in this space; even in the presence of established welfare states and publicly funded healthcare systems.

Despite strong reasons for the establishment and maintenance of such healthcare systems across the globe (see Chapter 3), and the role they have played in improving population health, health inequalities have persisted and grown. Firstly, therefore, we characterise the nature of health inequalities, the theories used to understand their causes and progress in the various means proposed for their alleviation. Thereafter, the potential of microcredit and impact bonds to act as an alternative, public health, means of acting on health – particularly of the least well-off – is considered.

This is important because the manifest outcomes of many microcredit and impact bond initiatives are, amongst other things, employment, income enhancement, improved education or housing, each of which has a relationship with health. The chapter concludes with another conceptual model; this time, to account for potential, identified latent outcomes associated with social finance and its impact on health and its social determinants.

Health inequalities: The road to social determinants

There is a long history of governments enacting social policies to improve the health of their nations. While different countries enacted

DOI: 10.4324/9781003305248-6

different policies at different times, in general, many of the major public health works, such as in sanitation and provision of a clean water supply, began around the time of the Industrial Revolution. However, the most ambitious and encompassing programme, to tackle not only poor health but also to avert the other identified social ills plaguing society, has been the creation of the welfare state. In the UK, for example, following the National Insurance Act of 1911, the Beveridge Report of 1942 outlined a comprehensive programme across education, social security, employment, health and housing to combat the five 'social evils' of the time: ignorance, want, idleness, disease and squalor. Thus, the Labour Government, elected in 1945, established programmes of social housing, universal secondary education, and, most notably with respect to health, the National Health Service (NHS). While many countries preceded or followed this with similar reforms, welfare state provision varies considerably between countries (3). Some countries, of course, also lack such social protection policies; including an NHS (see Chapter 3). In what follows, we primarily focus on the UK, which has a developed welfare state, to illustrate the road to the social determinants of health. The UK is considered a leader in health inequalities research and this context highlights the importance of the social determinants of health even where an established welfare state exists.

In the UK, a (now) internationally renowned report entitled *Inequalities in Health* (the Black Report) was commissioned in 1977 by the formerly named Department of Health and Social Security to investigate inequality in healthcare (4). The Black Report documented that while population health had improved since the implementation of the welfare state and the NHS, this improvement was not equal across all social classes; concurrent with increased population health were increased health inequalities, particularly in infant mortality rates and life expectancy.

Over time, further UK reports such as *The Health Divide* (the Whitehead Report), *Independent Enquiry into Inequalities in Health* (the Acheson Report) and *Fair Society, Healthy Lives* (the Marmot Review) helped establish the idea that health follows a social gradient (1,5,6). This observance has been termed 'social inequalities in health,' described as "systematic differences in health between different socioeconomic groups within a society" (7, p. 473). This definition speaks to the social rather than biological or genetic nature of health inequalities. Thus, importance is given to an individual's position in a social hierarchy for determining health. An influential study, of civil servants that began in 1967, based in Whitehall, helped demonstrate this effect (8–11). Those in the top social class, in terms of employment grade, had better health than those from the social class below. Furthermore, this followed a stepwise downward trend for each social class in turn in the study.

Consequently, across the world, a proliferation of research emerged in this area to try to understand the causes of ill health and health inequalities and to furnish the evidence base with interventions for their alleviation. For example, Professor Sir Michael Marmot, who led the UK Marmot Review (1), also chaired the World Health Organisation's (WHO's) Commission on the Social Determinants of Health that produced a report to support countries around the world address social factors that cause ill health and health inequalities (12). Although not always easy to obtain in consistent forms across high-income countries, disparities in life expectancy by various socio-economic indicators – such as education and poverty – have been shown in the USA (13), France (14), Germany (15) and Australia (16). By such classifications, disparities can be up to 10–15 years and, often, are even greater when analysed by ethnicity, with indigenous populations fairing even worse (17,18). These trends are also reflected in Hispanic populations (19,20). One of the most widely used approaches to counter the belief that health is determined by health services and behaviour is the 'rainbow' model of the main determinants of health, developed by Dahlgren and Whitehead (21,22), and shown in Figure 4.1.

To illustrate, ill health is typically explained through the behaviour that causes it, for example; smoking can cause lung disease. Conceptualising ill health in this way typically leads to 'downstream'

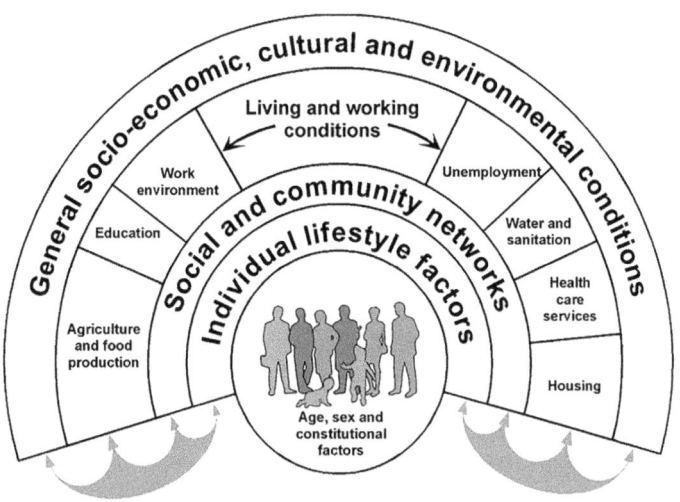

Source: adapted from Dahlgren and Whitehead, 1991

Figure 4.1 Dahlgren and Whitehead's rainbow model of the main determinants of health[1].

interventions focusing on individual pathologies and risk factors, such as smoking, diet, alcohol and exercise – often referred to as lifestyle factors. However, none of this tackles the underlying causes of such behaviours; the causes of the causes. To fully understand why an individual smokes requires consideration of social, economic and environmental factors; termed the social determinants of health. These determinants consider how different factors at the level of the individual, community and society interact to affect the conditions of daily life.

This way of thinking then leads to suggestions for more 'upstream' interventions to tackle the wider determinants of health, targeting the circumstances that lead to adverse behaviour, such as improving socio-economic status or neighbourhood conditions. We can now begin to see a place in this for social finance – but this represents new, and relatively unevidenced, thinking. Thus, downstream interventions continue to dominate even public health initiatives. Despite what may seem like challenges caused by this deficient evidencing of upstream interventions, this reflects the slow progress in our thinking about the public health role of upstream initiatives such as social finance. In the case of the UK, this can be seen over a 40-year time horizon through examination of recommendations proposed to alleviate health inequalities from the three landmark (commissioned) UK-based[2] national reports already referred to: the Black Report; the Acheson Report; and the Marmot Review (see Box 4.1).

In short, it could be argued that even the visionaries behind the creation of early universal healthcare systems in the 1930s and 1940s thought that, through clearing the backlog of sickness existing in their populations, health inequalities might be reduced, or even eliminated. The latter was obviously not the case, as we now know. Thus, in the 1970s, recommendations covered early years initiatives and health behaviours, although recognising that the latter takes place within social contexts. This had not progressed much by the 1990s, although acting on income inequality is more recognised. By the time of the Marmot Review, there is recognition of the role of wider social and economic environments. But even Marmot was criticised for lacking an evidence base (23). Coming full circle, this is in part why the main recommendations from the three reports are alike (24). Similar problems keep being identified but not acted upon or, at least, alleviated nor initiatives evaluated. The sparse nature of evidence led Bambra *et al.* (25, p. 290) to note that "it is particularly important to assemble evidence on the *mechanisms* by which policies may affect health; this will help identify points at which to intervene and will provide a framework for the development of new research."

Box 4.1   UK Reports on health inequalities

The Black Report, published in 1980, represents a landmark in overcoming the denial of a causal relationship between social class and health (26). On reviewing the evidence, a materialist/structural explanation considered class-related features of the UK socio-economic environment as being responsible for class differences in health along with cultural/behavioural explanations. In short, individual health-damaging behaviours, though important, are embedded within UK social structures (4). There were 37 recommendations emanating from the Report, but, broadly, covered: giving children a better start in life; encouraging good health among a larger proportion of the population by preventive and educational action; and, for disabled people, to reduce the risks of early death, to improve the quality of life whether in the community or in institutions, and as far as possible to reduce the need for the latter.

Reflecting a suspected lack of progress, the Acheson Report was commissioned and published in 1998 (5). Despite steps forward in conceptualising the determinants of health, Acheson reached similar conclusions to Black in showing continuing, and sometimes growing, disparities in health. The 39 steps aimed at reducing health inequalities focused on three areas as follows: all policies impacting on health should be evaluated in terms of their impact on health inequalities; high priority should be given to the health of families with children; and further steps should be taken to reduce income inequalities and improve the living standards of poor households. Only three of the 39 recommendations were concerned with the NHS, but were criticised for being unevidenced and uncosted (27–29).

Subsequent to Professor Sir Michael Marmot chairing the WHO report on the Social Determinants of Health – *Closing the Gap in a Generation* (12) – he was commissioned by the UK Government in 2008 to examine health inequalities within England and make corresponding evidence-based policy recommendations. The report *Fair Society, Healthy Lives* was published in 2010 (1). As previously, available evidence relating to health inequalities was reviewed and then utilised to propose recommendations related to six identified policy objectives: give every child the best start in life; enable all children, young people and adults to maximise their capabilities and have control over their lives; create fair employment and good work for all; ensure healthy standard of living for all; create and develop healthy and sustainable places and communities; strengthen the role and impact of ill health prevention.

This suggests that, due to the nature of upstream interventions and the distance from behaviours/health of individuals, straightforward causal relationships might be difficult to identify and isolate. It also highlights the need for further research work in the area of potential upstream interventions that could impact upon health. It is proposed here that microcredit and impact bonds could have roles to play as upstream interventions that impact on health; roles which we will now initially conceptualise and evidence.

Beyond healthcare and risk factors: A role for social finance?

Recognising that health policies alone cannot redress health inequalities has led to international and national movements to make health a focus in all policies. This requires intersectoral action. One prominent approach is 'Health in All Policies' (HiAP). The 'Helsinki Statement' on HiAP, released in 2013, called on governments to adopt inter-sectoral action on population health and health inequities[3] and prioritise action on the social determinants of health (31). A variety of HiAP approaches exist in countries across the world, including Australia, Finland, Norway, Denmark, Sweden, Iran, Kenya and Cuba (32). While there is a coherent HiAP narrative and pockets of progress, implementing a HiAP is challenging as it requires political will to facilitate cooperation across sectors and, overall, little appears to have substantively changed. This is important to bear in mind as we now consider the potential role and, of course, evidence for social finance, within the realms of social and economic policy, for improving living and working conditions.

Some impact bonds, as illustrated in Chapter 3, are explicitly health-focused, and even possess strong elements of public health. But, beyond these health service roles for impact bonds, there is a bigger picture to consider. That is, where the initiatives funded by impact bonds act as potential determinants of improved health and well-being, even where not setting out explicitly to do so (33). Indeed, many impact bonds would express their missions in other terms, such as through providing opportunities for people who would otherwise be long-term unemployed and access to stable homes for rough sleepers. Chapter 5 maps those impact bonds that set out to impact on health outcomes

The same logic can be applied to microfinance. Generally, the micro-finance literature focuses on the more-instrumental direct link between microfinance and health. As outlined in Chapter 3, and further evidenced in Chapter 7, this relationship focuses on financial products explicitly aimed at health (i.e. microinsurance) and improving access to healthcare (i.e. microfinance-plus). Yet there is a developing evidence base around

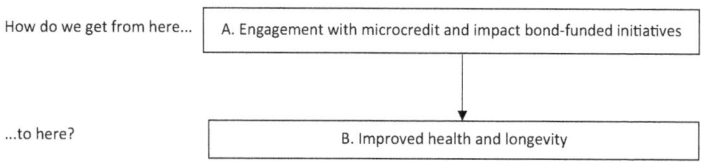

Figure 4.2 The causal chain of social finance and public health: getting from A to B?

microcredit, in and of itself, acting as a socioeconomic determinant of health (34,35). This conceptualisation sees microcredit provision as a 'non-obvious' public health measure as it possesses ability, through its lending and repayment mechanisms, to act on upstream determinants of health even if this is not a stated objective or mission of provision (which is typically around poverty alleviation or financial exclusion). This new role for microcredit will be developed in full in Chapter 6.

Given the aims of impact bonds and microcredit providers, it could be argued that this provides adequate justification for evaluating these forms of social finance in regard to their stated missions alone. However, with governments looking for new ways to fund public services, manage welfare, encourage intersectoral policymaking and also to new solutions for the sustained public health challenges outlined above, it will be important to be able to monitor the longer-term success (or otherwise) of such alternatives. But how might the evaluation of such policy initiatives be undertaken? If improvements in well-being were to be characterised as leading to enhanced health and longevity in the future, this then begs the question of how we get from A to B in Figure 4.2.

To answer this, we first need to establish the plausible mechanisms of getting from A to B, and then attempt to measure them. Some such mechanisms are more obvious than others. A simple model for an evaluation is built up in Figure 4.3.

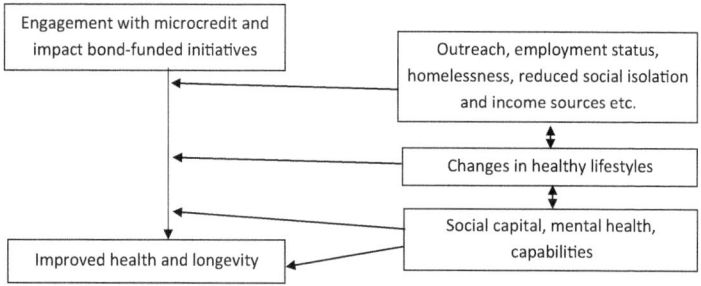

Figure 4.3 The causal chain of social finance and public health: towards final outcomes.

For now, the relationship in the first box in Figure 4.3 is posited because we know that not only income but also employment status, and by extension, homelessness, social isolation and other factors, are associated with health and well-being. The question is whether acting on these will then impact on the health of more vulnerable people and, thus, reduce health inequalities. Furthermore, with little political desire at present for (income) redistributive policies in many countries, impact bonds and microcredit could be considered as less-direct ways to achieve this. It may also decrease reliance on the welfare system and engender extra impacts from people helping themselves.

Other links are also plausible. On the face of it, it may seem that impact bonds and microcredit provide a possible solution to the chronic problem of worklessness[4] that exists in so many low-income communities. Indeed, this is why it is worth a try. However, it would require monitoring not only of income levels of intervention recipients, but also of whether such services reach those for whom they were initially intended. This is especially necessary in countries with well-established welfare systems through which some level of income support is already provided and may indeed militate against engagement with some such interventions, such as microcredit.

One may also question how it is the case that engaging with impact bond initiatives and microcredit could change the lifestyles of service recipients in ways consistent with ultimate health improvement. If health improvement were to follow in the long run, might we expect to observe changes in smoking behaviour, environment, diet, physical activity and the like in the interim? Again, this would require collection of data from service users over time on such aspects and comparison of these data with trends in the general population and also in equally deprived areas with no access to such interventions.

Completing this simple model, in many respects, initiatives funded via impact bonds and microcredit can rely on 'social capital,' the idea that, with a little help, a community can group together and make quite significant advances in improving itself. But does it also add to social capital? Again, such impacts on the wider community in terms of its cohesiveness can, to an extent, be measured (36,37). At the most basic level, do beneficiaries of impact bonds and microcredit stay in their communities or migrate from them? Likewise, the psychological health of individuals in such communities can also be tracked over time and measured against relevant comparators. Indeed, interventions to supplement income have been criticised for missing major opportunities to assess impacts on health outcomes (38,39). Going beyond what might be seen as narrower health outcomes, health researchers have been active in trying to operationalise Amartya Sen's notion of capabilities[5] (40) into parsimonious measures to be applied to study participants over time

(41,42) and aspects such as dignity and autonomy can be captured by measures of confidence and ego development from psychology (43,44).

All of the above mechanisms have been portrayed in what might seem like a rather quantitative 'model' linking, for example, income, money and enterprise to health and well-being. However, to gain a richer understanding of how impact bond-funded initiatives and microcredit can enhance people's lives, or what the barriers to success might be, rigorous qualitative research is also required to explain the links in the model through the personal stories of intervention recipients. Furthermore, the relationships may often not be as linear as portrayed by the arrows in the diagram. For example, one may first build social capital that then leads on to improvements in healthy lifestyles, leading through to ultimate health improvements. We will revisit such issues with more elaborate and evidence-based models later.

Conclusion

Meeting health and healthcare needs and reducing inequalities in health and well-being are fundamental roles of societies. Nevertheless, these challenges are persistent and stubborn both globally and within countries. Social finance is but one solution upon which policymakers seem to have converged across countries in recent years.

In richer countries, new thinking is emerging about 'other' (e.g. non-healthcare and even non-obvious) ways of acting on determinants of health and well-being. In lower-income countries, it is more about filling the gaps that publicly funded institutions and private companies (such as insurance companies) are not able or willing to enter, i.e. repairing aspects of market failure. But, the points about potential impacts on determinants of health also apply there. This convergence has manifested itself in the notion of social finance, sometimes in the form of microcredit, microinsurance or impact bonds, as a potential way forward in addressing social problems, poverty and, thus, in potentially impacting on health and well-being; either directly (through funding health services and community health initiatives) or indirectly (as non-healthcare entities impacting on health and well-being).

In short, in aiming to provide solutions to healthcare access and, as illustrated in this particular chapter, to other social challenges, social finance can act as a determinant of health and well-being. This leads us to a framework that opens the 'evaluative space' for social finance beyond financial payback and outreach, important though these may be. Our intention is that the framework we have begun to construct can be seen not only as outlining an agenda for research action but also as something to be further theorised and conceptualised through applied studies that we review in forthcoming chapters of this volume.

Notes

1 Reprinted from Public Health, vol. 199, Göran Dahlgren and Margaret Whitehead, The Dahlgren-Whitehead model of health determinants: 30 years on and still chasing rainbows, pages 20–24, Copyright (2021), with permission from Elsevier.
2 The Black Report was UK-wide, while the focus of the Acheson Report and the Marmot Review was England.
3 In certain countries (e.g. the UK), this term is often used interchangeably with health inequalities, defined as systematic differences in health between different social groups, such as the best and worst-off (30).
4 'Worklessness' is the rather trendy and non-specific term that does however serve a useful purpose of highlighting the issue of economic inactivity as well as unemployment. It is often used to refer to people who, it is claimed, are not seeking work, families in which no one is employed and communities with major problems of unemployment and economic inactivity, often experienced not only in high rates amongst the population at any one time but also over time and, on occasion, across generations.
5 Capabilities are the doings and beings that people can achieve if they want e.g. to eat nutritional meals or be educated. Functionings are a related concept, meaning realised capabilities.

References

1. Marmot M. Fair Society: Healthy Lives. *Strategic Review of Health Inequalities in England Post-2010.* 2010. (The Marmot Review).
2. Marmot M, Wilkinson RG. *Social Determinants of Health.* Second edition. Oxford University Press; 2006.
3. Bambra C. Going beyond The three worlds of welfare capitalism: regime theory and public health research. *Journal of Epidemiology & Community Health.* 2007;61(12):1098–1102.
4. Department of Health and Social Security. *Inequalities in Health.* London: Department of Health and Social Security; 1980. (The Black Report).
5. Acheson D. *Independent Enquiry into Inequalities in Health.* London: The Stationery Office; 1998.
6. Whitehead M. *The Health Divide: Inequalities in Health in the 1980s.* Health Education Council; 1987.
7. Whitehead M. A typology of actions to tackle social inequalities in health. *Journal of Epidemiology & Community Health.* 2007;61(6):473–478.
8. Marmot MG, Rose G, Shipley M, Hamilton PJ. Employment grade and coronary heart disease in British civil servants. *J Epidemiol Community Health (1978).* 1978;32(4):244–249.
9. Marmot MG, Stansfeld S, Patel C, North F, Head J, White I, et al. Health inequalities among British civil servants: the Whitehall II study. *The Lancet.* 1991;337(8754):1387–1393.
10. Davey Smith G, Shipley MJ, Rose G. Magnitude and causes of socio-economic differentials in mortality: further evidence from the Whitehall Study. *Journal of Epidemiology & Community Health.* 1990;44(4):265–270.
11. Marmot MG, Shipley MJ, Rose G. Inequalities in death – Specific explanations of a general pattern? *The Lancet.* 1984;1003–1006.

12. WHO. Closing the gap in a generation: health equity through action on the social determinants of health. Final report of the Commission on Social Determinants of Health. *World Health Organisation*. Commission on Social Determinants of Health; 2008. p. 253.

13. Singh GK, Lee H. Marked disparities in life expectancy by education, poverty level, occupation, and housing tenure in the United States, 1997–2014. *Int J MCH AIDS*. 2021;10(1):7–18.

14. Blanpain N. New data on life expectancy and standard of living in France. *N-IUSSP*. 2018.

15. Wenau G, Grigoriev P, Shkolnikov V. Socioeconomic disparities in life expectancy gains among retired German men, 1997–2016. *J Epidemiol Community Health*. 2019;73(7):605–611.

16. Welsh J, Bishop K, Booth H, Butler D, Gourley M, Law H, et al. *Inequalities in Life Expectancy in Australia according to Education Level: A Whole-of-Population Record Linkage Study*. Epidemiology; 2021.

17. Trewin D, Madden R. The Health and Welfare of Australia's Aboriginal and Torres Strait Islander Peoples 2005. *Commonwealth of Australia: Australian Bureau of Statistics*. Australian Institute of Health and Welfare; 2005.

18. Statistics Canada. Life expectancy of First Nations, Métis and Inuit household populations in Canada. 2019.

19. Bilal U, Cainzos-Achirica M, Cleries M, Santaeugènia S, Corbella X, Comin-Colet J, et al. Socioeconomic status, life expectancy and mortality in a universal healthcare setting: An individual-level analysis of >6 million Catalan residents. *Preventive Medicine*. 2019;123:91–94.

20. Bilal U, Alazraqui M, Caiaffa WT, Lopez-Olmedo N, Martinez-Folgar K, Miranda JJ, et al. Inequalities in life expectancy in six large Latin American cities from the SALURBAL study: an ecological analysis. *The Lancet Planetary Health*. 2019;3(12):e503–e510.

21. Dahlgren G, Whitehead M. The Dahlgren-Whitehead model of health determinants: 30 years on and still chasing rainbows. *Public Health*. 2021;199: 20–24.

22. Dahlgren G, Whitehead M. *Policies and Strategies to Promote Social Equity in Health*. Stockholm, Sweden: Institute for Futures Studies; 1991.

23. Bambra C, Smith KE, Garthwaite K, Joyce KE, Hunter DJ. A labour of Sisyphus? Public policy and health inequalities research from the Black and Acheson Reports to the Marmot Review. *Journal of Epidemiology & Community Health*. 2011;65(5):399–406.

24. Pickett KE, Dorling D. Against the organization of misery? The Marmot Review of health inequalities. *Social Science & Medicine*. 2010;71(7): 1231–1233.

25. Bambra C, Gibson M, Sowden A, Wright K, Whitehead M, Petticrew M. Tackling the wider social determinants of health and health inequalities: evidence from systematic reviews. *Journal of Epidemiology & Community Health*. 2010;64(4):284–291.

26. Blane D. An assessment of the Black Report's explanations of health inequalities. *Sociology of Health & Illness*. 1985;7(3):423–445.

27. Davey Smith G, Morris JN, Shaw M. The independent inquiry into inequalities in health. *BMJ*. 1998;317:1465–1466.

28. Birch S. The 39 steps: the mystery of health inequalities in the UK. *Health Economics.* 1999;8(4):301–308.

29. MacIntyre S. Reducing health inequalities: An action report. *Critical Public Health.* 1999;9(4):347–350.

30. Smith KE, Bambra C, Hill SE. Health Inequalities: Critical Perspectives. *Health Inequalities.* Oxford University Press; 2015.

31. WHO. *Health in All Policies: Helsinki Statement, Framework for Country Action: The 8th Global Conference on Health Promotion.* World Health Organization; 2014.

32. Cairney P, St Denny E, Mitchell H. The future of public health policymaking after COVID-19: a qualitative systematic review of lessons from Health in All Policies. *Open Res Europe.* 2021;1:23.

33. Iovan S, Lantz PM, Shapiro S. "Pay for success" projects: Financing interventions that address social determinants of health in 20 countries. *Am J Public Health.* 2018;108(11):1473–1477.

34. Ibrahim F, McHugh N, Biosca O, Baker R, Laxton T, Donaldson C. Microcredit as a public health initiative? Exploring mechanisms and pathways to health and wellbeing. *Social Science & Medicine.* 2021;270:113633.

35. McHugh N, Biosca O, Donaldson C. From wealth to health: Evaluating microfinance as a complex intervention. *Evaluation.* 2017;23(2):209–225.

36. Bynner JM, Paxton W. *The Asset-effect.* Institute for Public Policy Research; 2001.

37. Pronyk PM, Harpham T, Morison LA, Hargreaves JR, Kim JC, Phetla G, et al. Is social capital associated with HIV risk in rural South Africa? *Social Science & Medicine.* 2008;66(9):1999–2010.

38. Connor J, Rodgers A, Priest P. Randomised studies of income supplementation: A lost opportunity to assess health outcomes. *Journal of Epidemiology and Community Health (1979-).* 1999;53(11):725–730.

39. Ludbrook A, Porter K. Do interventions to increase income improve the health of the poor in developed economies and are such policies cost effective?: *Applied Health Economics and Health Policy.* 2004;3(2):115–120.

40. Sen A. Capability and Well-being. In: *The Quality of Life.* Oxford: Clarendon Press; 1993.

41. Coast J, Flynn TN, Natarajan L, Sproston K, Lewis J, Louviere JJ, et al. Valuing the ICECAP capability index for older people. *Social Science & Medicine.* 2008;67(5):874–882.

42. Al-Janabi H, Flynn TN, Coast J. Development of a self-report measure of capability wellbeing for adults: the ICECAP-A. *Qual Life Res.* 2012;21(1): 167–176.

43. Gilmore JM, Durkin K. A critical review of the validity of ego development theory and its measurement. *Journal of Personality Assessment.* 2001;77(3): 541–567.

44. Eriksson M. Validity of Antonovsky's sense of coherence scale: a systematic review. *Journal of Epidemiology & Community Health.* 2005;59(6):460–466.

Part 3
Evidence

5 Social finance ... *funding* health(care) services

Introduction

So far, we have outlined challenges facing the funding of health(care) services, the need to identify new initiatives to act on the determinants of health and, in broad terms, the potential role social finance could play in response. In the next three chapters, we evidence and discuss, in turn, the role of three specific forms of social finance – impact bonds, microcredit and microfinance-plus – in addressing these global health challenges. We begin with impact bonds.

Countries around the world contend with similar issues in relation to scarce public sector funding: how can we get more bang for our buck? How can we increase the amount of money available to pay for public and social services? How can we gain access to new sources of funding to pay for these services? While these questions are always a concern, they took on increased significance following the financial crisis of 2008 that led to a prolonged period of reduced public spending (or austerity) in the name of deficit reduction. In this context, there was a willingness to experiment with innovative new financing mechanisms. From the social investment sector, impact bonds, a form of Payment-by-Results (PbR), quickly came to prominence as a way to tackle social issues with the alluring promise of a "win-win-win" (1); more effective social services provided at less expense and risk to the public purse with the capability of generating profits for investors. Since the world's first impact bond was announced in the United Kingdom (UK) in 2010 – the Peterborough Social Impact Bond that aimed to reduce reoffending at HMP Peterborough Prison (2) – the use of impact bonds has grown throughout the world. Impact bonds fall into two main categories – social impact bonds (SIBs) and development impact bonds (DIBs). At the time of writing, the Brookings Institution identifies 225 impact bonds (210 SIBs and 15 DIBs) contracted in 37 countries (i.e. low-, middle- and high-income countries) (3). These impact bonds have raised approximately $462.68 million

DOI: 10.4324/9781003305248-8

dollars in upfront capital for the funding of interventions that operate across six main sectors: social welfare, employment, health, education, criminal justice, and environment and agriculture. However, despite offering a new way of funding social and public services, there exist numerous critiques – technical and ideological – of this form of social finance.

This chapter will first introduce impact bonds and the arguments for and against them, before focusing on a particular subset of impact bonds – health impact bonds. As outlined in Chapters 3 and 4, impact bonds are a new way to fund health(care) services and interventions and potentially act on determinants of health. However, we do not have a clear sense of their nature and reach in regards to health. In the second half of the chapter, we present the results of a mapping exercise that provides a clearer sense of how many health impact bonds exist, where they operate in the health system, what they focus on and what indicators trigger payments. We then discuss whether health impact bonds have untapped potential or represent a broken promise and if they target the source, or effects, of the problem.

What are impact bonds?

Social impact bonds (SIBs)

What are SIBs?

The UK led the development of the first category of impact bonds – SIBs. SIBs sometimes go by other names in different countries, for example, pay for success (PFS) in the USA and social benefit bonds (SBB) in Australia, different SIB models exist and the SIB model can diverge between theory and practice. In a general SIB model, there are typically five main types of stakeholder: an outcome payer; an intermediary; investor(s); service providers and an evaluator. We also highlight service users who despite receiving the intervention are generally not involved in the design of a SIB. The specific roles of, and relationships between, these different stakeholders are outlined in Table 5.1 and illustrated by Figure 5.1 (adapted from Liebman and Sellman (4)). In Figure 5.1, the blue solid arrows indicate the main financial relationships, and indeed flows, prior to delivery of the intervention, whereby investors transfer money to the intermediary, which, on having agreed targets to trigger payments with service providers, then pass on the finance to said providers who spend the money on interventions for service users. The green dotted, and orange solid, arrows show the main relationships and financial flows following the evaluation of the intervention's performance. For that evaluation,

Table 5.1 Social impact bond stakeholders and roles

Stakeholder	Role
Intermediary	Raises funds to pay for the delivery of an intervention from *investors* and contracts, and provides this funding as upfront capital to, *service providers* to deliver an intervention.
Outcome payer	Typically, a government agency or public body repays the principal (i.e. the initial funding) plus interest to the *investor(s)* through the *intermediary* if agreed upon outcomes are met as measured by the *evaluator*. The *outcome payer* is not required to make payments if the *service provider* fails to achieve a base level of agreed outcomes.
Investor(s)	Private, philanthropic and/or social *investors* provide the upfront funding (i.e. principal) for an intervention. Whether the *investor* receives repayments and the size of repayments depends on the performance of the intervention against agreed upon outcomes.
Service provider(s)	One or more private, public and/or third sector *service providers* deliver an intervention to a target population (i.e. *service users*).
Evaluator	Typically, an independent *evaluator* measures the impact of the intervention on *service users*.

data on outcomes (green dotted arrow) are transferred to evaluators who, in turn, inform the outcome payer via the intermediary. This then triggers outcome-based payments (orange solid arrows) from the outcome payer back to investors via the intermediary.

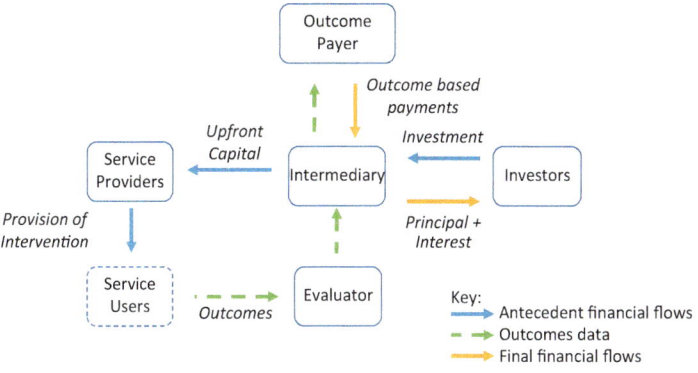

Figure 5.1 Impact bond model.

Why use SIBs?

SIBs emerged from PbR contracts introduced in the UK as a way for government to pay providers of outsourced public services on the achievement of agreed upon and measured outcomes (5). SIBs extend traditional PbR models. Unlike PbR contracts where service providers receive payment retrospectively, in a SIB, service providers receive payment for the intervention upfront from money raised by the intermediary from investors (6). This potentially increases the pool of service providers able to offer an intervention and transfers the financial risk of the intervention from service providers to investors. In theory, the outcome payer (i.e. government) pays for a successful SIB from future savings ostensibly accrued from the resultant benefits of the intervention. In harnessing new sources of capital to fund the upfront costs of social interventions and removing the risk of public money being spent on failed interventions, SIBs represent a new form of public-private partnership focused on social interventions rather than physical infrastructure projects (7–9).

As SIBs provide secure upfront funding and focus on outcomes they are considered as particularly well suited to funding preventive initiatives (10,11). This is also thought to encourage more innovation in service delivery (11) and could overcome a perception of the public sector as being too risk averse and inflexible to address wicked social problems (12,13). The preventive focus also explains why the outcome payer – government – is ostensibly able to make SIB payments from future savings. Linking financial returns to outcomes is also expected to increase performance management as investors are only paid if an independent evaluator verifies that agreed upon outcomes are met (9). This can enhance the accountability and transparency of public sector expenditures and improve the performance of social interventions (14,15). In this way, SIBs introduce market rigour into the provision of public services.

Development impact bonds (DIBs)

What are DIBs?

DIBs adapt the model of SIBs for the financing of public services in low- and middle-income countries (LMICs). As such, the DIB model resembles that of the SIB (see Table 5.1 and Figure 5.1). While DIBs are specific to LMICs, this is not their distinguishing feature; SIBs also exist in LMICs (for example, The Innovation Fund Impact Bond in South Africa that focuses on early childhood development). Instead what separates a SIB from a DIB is the outcome payer.

Whereas a government agency or body is the outcome payer in a SIB, an external third party, such as an aid agency, philanthropic foundation or charity, funds the DIB instead of, or alongside, the domestic government (16).

Why use a DIB?

DIBs emerged from discussions between the Centre for Global Development, a non-profit think tank focused on international development, and Social Finance, the intermediary organisation responsible for structuring the world's first SIB – the Peterborough SIB (17). Like SIBs which have their roots in PbR contracts, DIBs evolved from other forms of financing mechanisms used in LMIC countries to fund social programmes which link payments to results such as Results Based Aid (e.g. Cash on Delivery Aid) and Results-Based Financing (e.g. Output-Based Aid) (16,17). The funding, and financial risk, of interventions generally sits with the government in the former and service providers in the latter. DIBs, like SIBs, transfer the upfront funding and risk to investors.

A 'coordination problem' that impedes the funding and scaling-up, of socially valuable services exists in LMICs (16). Service providers struggle to access low-cost capital for interventions that could potentially generate needed social outcomes, investors have an unwillingness to provide this type of capital and donors typically provide input-focused financing that could stifle innovative approaches for generating outcomes. DIBs could potentially overcome these issues due to their focus on outcomes and improved performance management from linking financial returns to meeting outcome targets.

Finally, similar to SIBs, DIBs should, in theory, result in a more efficient use of public funds and save the domestic government money. However, DIBs could have additional advantages. Domestic governments collaborating with external third parties as outcome payers generate new and additional sources of funding and, in theory, this should also result in the more efficient use of donor funding.

Technical and ideological challenges

An interesting facet of impact bonds is that proponents and critics broadly congregate in two main camps. Policy actors, think tanks, non-profits, and corporate organisations are generally favourable towards impact bonds for the reasons outlined above (12,18), while a more 'cautionary narrative' is apparent within academic literature (10). This caution relates to broad issues: technical and ideological challenges. These challenges are more established in relation to SIBs as this form of impact bond is more developed and widespread. However, as DIBs share similar principles to SIBs, the challenges are broadly applicable to impact bonds in general.

Technical challenges

Technical challenges correspond to four broad, overlapping, areas: outcomes, transaction costs, governance and goals, and innovation.

Outcomes

While focusing on outcomes to trigger payments, instead of inputs or outputs, is generally welcome, this raises a number of issues in relation to measurement, perverse incentives, attribution, long-term effects and value for money.

Social outcomes are difficult to measure. Validated outcome measures may not exist with proxies required. There can also be many different ways to measure the same outcome and/or a lack of good quality data can make it difficult to choose outcomes (16,19,20). While specifying and selecting the most appropriate outcome measure(s) is a key part of any evaluation, there is added significance when outcomes trigger payments. The risk is the creation of perverse incentives: selecting outcome measures that are easiest to define and measure, gaming practices that involve either selecting individuals with less need ('creaming') and/or focusing on the most treatable ('cherry picking') (6,21,22). With social interventions, pinpointing what exactly led to the observed outcome is notoriously difficult (i.e. the attribution problem). Social, unlike clinical, interventions generate behavioural responses, increasing the complexity of the casual chain (i.e. the cause-effect relationship) between the intervention and outcome, and environmental and contextual factors could, unknowingly, impact on the agreed-upon outcomes (13,23). Certain outcomes may only be sustained with the continuation of an intervention (22). As an impact bond contract is time-limited, there is a risk that long-term effects of a successful impact bond will be undone following the intervention's withdrawal. Lastly, there is limited evidence that impact bonds offer value for money, in terms of their cost-effectiveness, or result in better outcomes for service users compared to the direct public financing of public services (in the case of SIBs) or Results-Based Financing (RBF) or Results-Based Aid (RBA) approaches (in the case of DIBs) (15,16). There are different reasons for this. In general, there is a lack of evaluation studies and publicly available information. Specifically, in relation to DIBs, only a relatively small number of impact bonds have reached the stage of paying investors based on the achievement of outcomes.

Transaction costs

Impact bonds have high transaction costs (24), particularly in relation to their design and contracting arrangements. The number of stakeholders involved and the need to reach an agreement that satisfies all parties makes this a complex process requiring a significant amount of expertise as well as time and money. Decisions are required around, for example: the number and selection of outcomes; the timing of outcome payments; the level of outcome(s) that trigger payments; the length of the impact bond; the choice of intervention(s); the number, and type of, service providers and investors. The multi-stakeholder relationships (see Table 5.1 and Figure 5.1) also require multiple contracts. In the field, Oroxom et al. (16), for example, highlight that the design and contracting of a DIB can take one to three years. This complexity is also thought to rule out many smaller third-sector organisations from acting as service providers as they do not have the required systems, expertise or capacity to manage this form of social investment (23). This could dilute the claim that the fronting of capital will increase the pool of service providers available. Moreover, hopes for a more generic contracting mechanism for impact bonds that reduces transaction costs have dissipated due to the diversity of impact bonds and stakeholders involved (25).

Governance and goals

Outsourcing public and social service provision can reduce public and democratic accountability (20). Typically, government bodies or agencies directly provide public and social services or commission them from external providers. With impact bonds, the involvement of additional stakeholders increases the distance between provider and government. This increases the level of asymmetric information in the relationship between different stakeholders, diminishing governments' ability to provide effective oversight and there is evidence of intermediaries and investors having prominent roles in the design and oversight of impact bonds (2,7,22,26). A lack of public reporting, particularly from planned but not implemented impact bonds, exacerbates this issue. For example, DIBs planned in Nigeria and Mozambique for sleeping sickness prevention and nutrition, respectively, were deferred following design and contracting negotiations without the reasons being made clear (16). Intermediaries and investors do not necessarily have the same goals as government. Consequently, impact bonds could increase the risk of policy and service fragmentation (12,16,27). The risk is that interventions deemed good candidates for an impact bond crowd-out interventions that would better serve government priorities.

Innovation

Evidence from designed and implemented impact bonds weakens the claim that impact bonds stimulate innovative service delivery through the focus on outcomes. There is a paradox built into the impact bond model (6). The aim of investors providing upfront capital to service providers to achieve pre-specified outcomes is to liberate service providers. However, investors, even social investors, do not want to see interventions fail. In practice, SIBs are generally based on evidence-based interventions rather than innovative new approaches and evidence exists of reduced flexibility caused by the involvement of private capital which brings increased oversight and administrative costs (22,28). Such approaches are adopted to mitigate uncertainty around the achievement of outcomes and to also reduce the cost of SIBs through lower rates of returns to investors (6). However, this comes at the expense of innovation. This also highlights how SIB models can differ between countries as, for example, the rhetoric around pay-for-success projects in the USA is, generally, always about the use of evidence-based interventions (8).

Evidence exists of the government underwriting part, or the full cost, of the impact bond rather than transferring the financial risk to investors. For example, investors in two SIBs in Canada and Australia, respectively, were offered partial protection of their initial investment and one investor in the Cameroon Cataract Bond (a DIB) was offered full capital protection if the intervention failed to meet agreed targets (16,27). Arguments for offering this protection range from signalling confidence in the intervention to building the impact bond sector, but critics see this as the public sector subsiding for private investors (29). Offering financial guarantees also risks introducing moral hazard into the impact bonds process as stakeholders will know that the government will incur the cost of any failure.

Ideological challenges

Ideological challenges relate to two overlapping issues: the portrayal of impact bonds as an ideology-free, apolitical and technical response to a social problem and their role in the financialisation of society and commodification of service users.

Ideology-free and apolitical

Impact bonds receive unusual levels of cross-party political support, which leads to their conception as an ideology-free, apolitical and technical response to a social problem. In the UK, the Labour Government first introduced PbR in welfare provision in 2009 and then announced the world's first SIB in 2010. The SIB model was then expanded and financially supported by the Conservative-Liberal Democrats Coalition UK Government (2010–2015) and the subsequent Conservative UK Government (13,23). A similar situation unfolded in the USA. Introduced pay-for-success bills received bipartisan support in both houses of Congress (30). An American Congressional official described the reasons for this support: "the Republicans like this because it lets the private sector get access to public social welfare dollars and the Democrats like it because it might increase public investment in social welfare" (31). The ability of impact bonds to respond to a wide and varied audience, particularly one not always known for finding common ground, points to their strategic ambiguity (15). However, this ideology-free conception is challenged by those viewing impact bonds as epitomising the encroachment of the market and principles of privatisation into social policy (13,18,32); particularly when impact bonds continue to receive support despite limited evidence that they fulfil their varied promises.

Financialisation and commodification

Arguments exist that impact bonds are further evidence of the financialisation of everyday life. The narrative around impact bonds is exemplified by a description of DIBs: "DIBs transform social problems into 'investible' opportunities by monetizing the benefits of tackling social problems" (17, p. 7). For critics of SIBs this monetisation of social problems is seen as a 'boundary shift,' qualitatively altering the character of public and social services (13). The end goal of service provision becomes about profit maximisation rather than helping service users because it is intrinsically a good thing to do. There are similar fears with DIBs. For example, in the early stages of the Mozambique nutrition DIB, concerns were raised that "the project could be perceived as investors making money off of poor and malnourished people" (16, p. 20). How impact bonds affect service provision is a concern, but arguably of greater worry is the impact on service users.

The impact bond model can marginalise service users. Typically, service users are excluded from the design of impact bonds leaving them voiceless and through the monetisation of outcomes they are transformed from service users into customers without consumer sovereignty as they lack choice over suppliers (9,18). This also results in their commodification; they become a potential source of revenue (13,18,23,26). There is some softening of critiques. For example, for the reasons outlined above impact bonds may be unsuitable for transformative interventions that aim to empower individuals but could be suitable for technical interventions that only require relatively simple behaviour change (18). Likewise, the financialising nature of SIBs may not be all consuming, with some evidence that different stakeholders can offer pushback and that context is important (33). However, this belief was tempered somewhat by these same authors recognising that "SIB's neoliberal logic privileges financial gains" (33, p. 828).

Health impact bonds

As outlined in Chapter 3, impact bonds are a new way of funding health (care) services and interventions. Yet, despite recognition of impact bonds operating in the health sector (3) there is no agreed upon definition of a health impact bond. Consequently, we do not have a clear sense of their nature and reach in the health system. This is even more important as impact bonds have the potential to act on health through interventions funded in non-health sectors (see Chapter 4). The rest of the chapter focuses on health impact bonds. First, we introduce health impact bonds and the arguments for and against them. We then present the results of a mapping exercise that provides a clearer sense of how many health impact bonds exist, where they operate in the health system, what they focus on and what indicators trigger payments. The outcome of this mapping exercise raises questions about the transformative nature of such an innovation as reflected in questions such as: what has been the rate of growth in their use over time; to what extent are genuine health outcomes used as a basis for triggering payments and what might this say for policy evaluation of bonds; which health issues are addressed by such bonds and does this meet with or distort priorities; and how are issues of sustainability (beyond the bond) addressed.

What are health impact bonds?

Health impact bonds represent the extension and adaptation of the impact bond model to the area of health. Despite the limited scholarship in this area, there is diversity in the conceptualisation of these types of bonds.

Health impact bonds are broadly framed around the funding of prevention activities (34,35). However, prevention is rarely explicitly defined and different authors focus on impact bonds in different areas of the health system: healthcare (7), the health sector (27), non-communicable diseases (35) and public health and the social determinants of health (8,36). This diversity of definitions makes it difficult to provide a clear sense of how many health impact bonds exist, where in the health system they operate and what they focus on. For example,

Hulse et al. (35) identify 11 impact bonds in eight different countries that focus on non-communicable diseases (e.g. cancer, diabetes, cardiovascular diseases and mental disorders). While Iovan et al. (36) find that all 82 pay-for-success projects launched in 20 different countries through 2017, map onto the World Health Organisation's (WHO) conceptual framework of the social determinants of health. The authors argue that this implies all funded projects, in some way, could improve health outcomes by acting on structural (e.g. employment, education, income) or intermediary (e.g. healthcare, behavioural risk factors) determinants of health. These studies both differ from, for example, the publicly available Government Outcomes Lab Impact Bond Dataset (37) that, at the time of writing, identifies 35 health impact bonds across 17 countries ranging from the UK to Russia and The Democratic Republic of the Congo.

Why are health impact bonds needed?

Similar arguments exist for health impact bonds as for impact bonds in general. For example, concerns about the sustainability of health systems that stem from fiscal constraints and increased demands for health services, the need to use resources more efficiently and the gradual implementation of market-based reforms in different areas of health systems (7,12,27,34). This has led to SIBs, for example, being promoted by organisations such as the WHO (38) to finance responses to non-communicable diseases. However, there exist rationales for using impact bonds that are also unique to health.

The development of methodologies in public health to calculate the probability, risk and uncertainty of illness and the likely impact of preventive responses could facilitate the use of impact bonds in health (34). Additionally, where health systems tend to focus on healthcare rather than prevention, such as the USA, impact bonds could help attract funding for social instead of medical interventions (8,30). While these are persuasive arguments, technical and ideological challenges also exist for impact bonds in health.

Challenges to health impact bonds

There are three main technical-related challenges specified in the literature. First, there is limited evidence of health impact bonds effectiveness and efficiency. Hulse et al. (35) find that only three of 11 impact bonds identified as targeting non-communicable diseases are meeting their target outcomes. Reasons for this relate, in part, to interventions not having a strong evidence base. Lack of evidence-based interventions was also identified as a concern among pay-for-success projects targeting different social determinants of health (8). Second, there are issues with health impact bonds not publicly disclosing their performance making it difficult to ascertain how an impact bond has performed (35). Lastly, the level of financial risk involved appears off-putting for mainstream financial investors, with most investors in health impact bonds being from foundations or third-sector organisations (27). To attract mainstream financial investors, full financial risk is not transferred to them, with allowances made for early termination and the offer of financial protection when outcomes are not met. Consequently, public priorities may be distorted to align with the investors' interests rather than public interest. In addition to these issues, discussed explicitly in relation to health impact bonds, authors working on this area also refer to the other technical challenges that impact bonds, in general, encounter.

Health impact bonds are not an ideology-free and apolitical response to a social problem. Instead, there is recognition that as health impact bonds commodify the health risk profiles of services users they are part of marketisation processes already apparent within health systems (34). However, there is some disagreement about how the introduction of a profit motive impacts government decision-making and the potential of trading health impact bonds.

While some express concerns that a profit motive could distort government priorities and spending (12), others view heath impact bonds as a catalyst for government spending on prevention (36,39). Second, while a secondary market to enable the trading of impact bonds has not yet emerged this is viewed as a possibility which could attract further investors (2,40). However, concerns exist about the social implications of this in relation to public health, specifically that trading health risks would negatively shift public health priorities (34) and lead to further separation from the service beneficiary, in terms of caring about the outcomes of service provision.

Mapping health impact bonds

The remainder of this chapter presents a mapping exercise that documents the reach and nature of health impact bonds. We begin by outlining the mapping exercise process – defining health impact bonds, developing a conceptual framework, data extraction, screening and synthesis approach – before presenting and discussing results.

Defining a health impact bond

To identify health impact bonds we utilise the WHO's (41) definition of health policies as decisions, plans and actions undertaken to achieve specific health goals within a society. Consequently, we define a health impact bond as one that must have at least one health indicator that triggers payment to the investor. We use the four domains stated in the WHO's Global Reference list of 100 Core Health Indicators (42): *health status, risk factors, service coverage and health systems. Health status* indicators act as a proxy for health outcomes with *risk factors, service coverage and health systems* providing insight on the inputs, processes and outputs that could lead to a change in outcomes. For included impact bonds, we also note whether they feature *non-health indicators*. Thus, we exclude those impact bonds that include indicators related to the social (or non-medical) determinants of health only. But our definition still recognises that impact bonds have the potential to impact on health through the social determinants of health (36) and will include those impact bonds in non-health sectors as long as they feature one health indicator. We also code included impact bonds to sub-domains of the respective indicators: mortality, morbidity, well-being (*health status*); nutrition, behaviour, environment, non-communicable diseases (*risk factors*); reproductive, mental health, non-communicable diseases screening, eye, HIV (*service coverage*); and inputs, outputs (*health systems*).

Conceptual framework of health impact bonds

The health indicators form the core part of our conceptual framework of health impact bonds (see Figure 5.2). We further conceptualise included health impact bonds within the health system by extending the conceptual framework applied by Thomson et al. (43). First, we conceptualise interventions using definitions of different *levels of prevention and care*. Specifically, primordial, primary, secondary and tertiary prevention and primary and secondary healthcare (44,45). Second, for each level of the intervention, we categorise the *delivery mechanisms*: fiscal, regulation, education, preventive treatment, screening, ongoing treatment, rehabilitation, general practice, community services, hospitals or clinics. Third, we identify the *policy domain* of the intervention as health (e.g. physical, mental health) and/or non-health (e.g. housing, unemployment). Finally, we categorise the *target population* of the intervention as population or high-risk only groups (46). Figure 5.2 illustrates the interactions between *levels of prevention and care, delivery mechanisms, policy domains, target populations* and *health indicators*; see Box 5.1 for the definitions underpinning the conceptual framework.

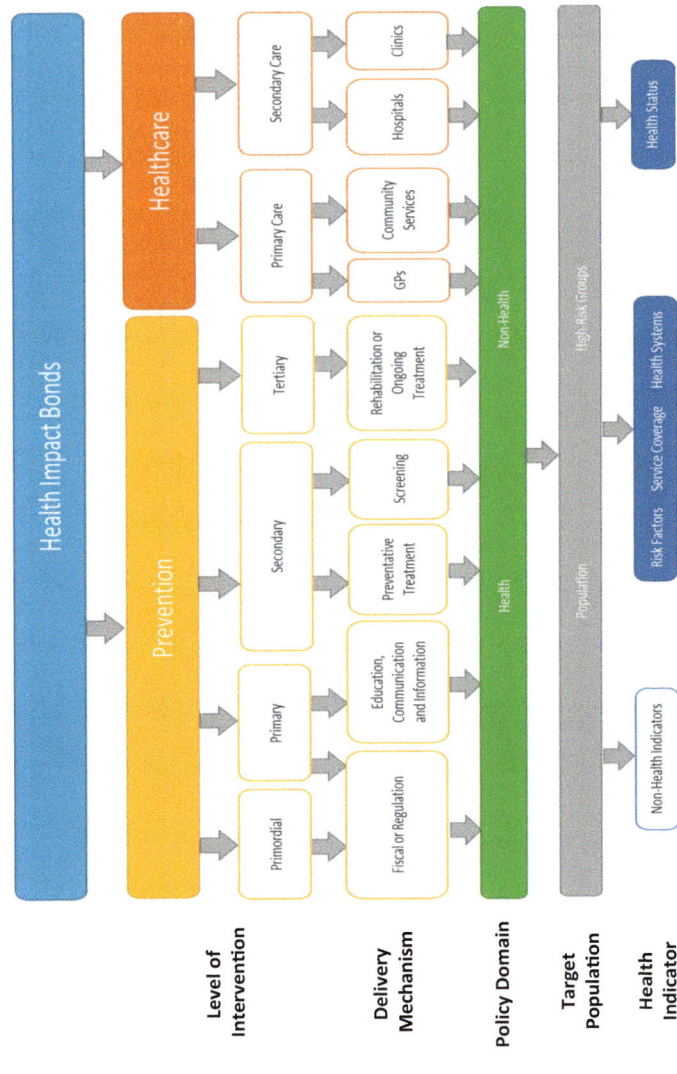

Figure 5.2 Conceptual framework of health impact bonds.

Box 5.1 Definitions underpinning the conceptual framework

Health policies

Decisions, plans, and actions undertaken to achieve specific health goals within a society.

Health indicators

Health status: indicators relating to mortality, morbidity and well-being.

Risk factors: indicators relating to nutrition, behaviour, violence and environment (e.g. pollution, sanitation, etc.).

Service coverage: indicators relating to different areas of service coverage (e.g. reproductive, non-communicable diseases, mental health, etc.).

Health systems: indicators relating to health system inputs (e.g. health infrastructure and workforce) and outputs (e.g. service access, availability, quality and safety).

Levels of prevention

Primordial prevention: strategies to prevent or inhibit the development and establishment of health risk factors.

Primary prevention: strategies to reduce the incidence of disease by reducing health risk exposures.

Secondary prevention: aims to diagnose and treat disease before symptoms occur.

Tertiary prevention: is concerned with reducing the effects of an ongoing disease or injury.

Level of healthcare

Primary care: relates to individuals' first point of contact with the healthcare system (e.g. general practice).

Secondary care: is when individuals require more specialised expertise (e.g. hospitals).

Target populations

Population approach: targets the whole population.
High-risk approach: targets those most at risk only.

Sources: WHO (41,42), Porta (44), Saltman et al. (45) and Rose (46).

Data extraction

We extracted data on impact bonds from the Government Outcomes (GO) Lab Impact Bond Dataset (37). This dataset is part of the International Network for Data on Impact and Government Outcomes (INDIGO) initiative that relies on individuals and organisations voluntarily sharing their data. We selected the 1st of March 2022 as our cut-off date for analysis. At this date, the wider dataset includes 225 impact bonds. We verified this total number via the Brooking Institution Global Impact Bond Database (47) that also reported 225 impact bonds at this date. Unlike the GO Lab Impact Bond Dataset, the Brookings Institution Global Impact Bond Database is not publicly available; so, it was not used to extract data on impact bonds.

Screening

From an initial screening of the GO Lab Impact Bond Dataset we identified and extracted data of 78 impact bonds which could possibly be categorised as health impact bonds. Of these, 27 required more information to make a decision. To identify further information we searched the Social Finance Impact Bond Global Database (48), other impact bond reviews (28,35,36) and, when necessary, searched for publicly available sources of data on specific impact bonds via Google. Two reviewers then independently categorised the impact bonds and discussed the results. Following this process, we identified 58 health impact bonds.

We extracted data on: name; delivery location; policy sector; capital raised; intervention; target population; target outcomes; and stakeholders. To verify the accuracy, we cross-checked the extracted data from the included health impact bonds with the Social Finance Impact Bond Global Database (48) and with other impact bond reviews (28,35,36). Following this verification, extracted data were categorised using the conceptual framework in Figure 5.2. Two reviewers undertook this process independently and then discussed results to arrive at a final categorisation.

Synthesis of results

The narrative synthesis summarises the identified health impact bonds in general and then by high-level policy domain (i.e. health or non-health). Online Appendix Table 5.1 provides a list of all 58 health impact bonds, summarised results by domain in relation to countries, (types of) indicators, level of intervention and target population in Tables 5.2–5.5. Our synthesis draws primarily on Tables 5.2–5.5. We also present three

Table 5.2 Number of health impact bonds by domain and country

Domain		No. of HIBs	Countries													Multi-country (NGA; COD; MLI)	PRT
			UK	USA	AUS	JPN	RUS	CMR	KHM	CAN	ETH	FIN	IND	ISR	KEN		
Health	Control of Infectious Diseases	1	1	-	-	-	-	-	-	-	-	-	-	-	-	-	-
	Mental Health	8	5	1	1	-	-	1	-	-	-	-	-	-	-	-	-
	Physical Health	17	4	2	-	3	3	-	-	1	-	1	-	1	-	1	1
	Reproductive Health	6	-	2	-	-	-	1	-	-	1	-	1	-	1	-	-
	Sanitation	1	-	-	-	-	-	-	1	-	-	-	-	-	-	-	-
	Substance Misuse	2	1	1	-	-	-	-	-	-	-	-	-	-	-	-	-
	Sub-Total	*35*	*11*	*6*	*1*	*3*	*3*	*2*	*1*	*1*	*1*	*1*	*1*	*1*	*1*	*1*	*1*
Non-Health	Carers	1	1	-	-	-	-	-	-	-	-	-	-	-	-	-	-
	Criminal Justice	1	-	-	1	-	-	-	-	-	-	-	-	-	-	-	-
	Education	2	1	-	1	-	-	-	-	-	-	-	-	-	-	-	-
	Housing	14	11	1	2	-	-	-	-	-	-	-	-	-	-	-	-
	Unemployment	1	1	-	-	-	-	-	-	-	-	-	-	-	-	-	-
	Young People	4	4	-	-	-	-	-	-	-	-	-	-	-	-	-	-
	Sub-Total	*23*	*18*	*1*	*4*	*0*	*0*	*0*	*0*	*0*	*0*	*0*	*0*	*0*	*0*	*0*	*0*
	Total	**58**	**29**	**7**	**5**	**3**	**3**	**2**	**1**	**1**	**1**	**1**	**1**	**1**	**1**	**1**	**1**

HIBs=Health impact bonds.

case studies of health (SIB and DIB) and non-health (SIB) domain impact bonds (see Boxes 5.2–5.4).

Results

In total, we identified 58 health impact bonds across 17 countries throughout the world (see Table 5.2). The UK contained the most impact bonds (29) followed by the USA (7) and Australia (5). Only two additional countries contained >2 impact bonds: Japan (3) and Russia (3). Health impact bonds are located in eight high-income (UK, USA, Australia, Japan, Canada, Finland, Israel, Portugal) and in nine middle- (Russia, Cameroon, Cambodia, India, Kenya and Nigeria) and low-income (Ethiopia, Mali, Democratic Republic of Congo) countries. While the spread of health impact bonds across countries of differing income levels is fairly even, they are proportionally more common in high-income countries where over 80% are located. Reflecting, their relatively recent development only seven of these impact bonds are DIBs, with Cameroon (2) having the highest number (see Online Appendix Table 5.1).

We find health impact bonds across two main domains – health (35) and non-health (23) – each of which contains six sub-domains (see Table 5.3). Of the 58 health impact bonds: three have health status indicators only; 29 have health status indicators with a combination of other health indicator(s) and/or non-health indicator(s); 12 have other health indicator(s) and non-health indicator(s); and 14 have other health indicator(s) only (see Table 5.3). Across all health impact bonds there are 136 health indicators: 51% are health systems indicators; 26% health status indicators; 15% service coverage indicators; and 8% risk factor indicators (see Table 5.4). Only four types of health indicators are used >10 times: health systems-outputs (61); health status-well-being (24); health status-morbidity (11); and service coverage-mental health (11). There are no health status-mortality indicators.

Twenty-nine impact bonds fund interventions that are prevention only, two are healthcare only and 27 are a combination of prevention and healthcare (see Table 5.3). Table 5.5 shows that the most frequent level of intervention is tertiary prevention-rehabilitation or ongoing treatment (60%) followed by primary prevention-education, communication and information (24%). No interventions are primordial prevention, primary prevention-fiscal or primary prevention-regulation. Within healthcare, 79% of interventions are primary care-community services and 21% are secondary care. There are no primary care GP interventions. Finally, 49 health impact bonds target high-risk groups and nine are population-wide (see Table 5.3).

Table 5.3 Number of health impact bonds by domain, indicators, level of intervention and target population

Domain		No. of HIBs	Indicators				Level of Intervention			Target Population	
			HS Only	HS & OHI &/or Non-HI	OHI & Non-HI	OHI only	P only	HC only	P & HC	Pop.	HR
Health	Control of Infectious Diseases	1	–	1	–	–	–	–	1	–	1
	Mental Health	8	2	4	1	1	–	1	7	–	8
	Physical Health	17	1	5	3	8	5	1	11	6	11
	Reproductive Health	6	–	3	–	3	–	–	6	3	3
	Sanitation	1	–	–	–	1	1	–	–	–	1
	Substance Misuse	2	–	–	2	–	–	–	2	–	2
	Sub-Total	*35*	*3*	*13*	*6*	*13*	*6*	*2*	*27*	*9*	*26*
Non-Health	Carers	1	–	–	1	–	1	–	–	–	1
	Criminal Justice	1	–	–	–	1	1	–	–	–	1
	Education	2	–	2	–	–	2	–	–	–	2
	Housing	14	–	9	5	–	14	–	–	–	14
	Unemployment	1	–	1	–	–	1	–	–	–	1
	Young People	4	–	4	–	–	4	–	–	–	4
	Sub-Total	*23*	*0*	*16*	*6*	*1*	*23*	*0*	*0*	*0*	*23*
	Total	**58**	**3**	**29**	**12**	**14**	**29**	**2**	**27**	**9**	**49**

HIBs=Health impact bonds; HS=Health status; OHI=Other health indicators; Non-HI=Non-health indicators; P=Prevention; HC=Healthcare; Pop.=Population-wide; HR= High-risk.

Table 5.4 Types of health indicators

| | | Health Indicators — Health Status | | | Risk Factors | | | | Service Coverage | | | | | | Health Systems | | | |
| | | | | | | | | | | | | | | | | | | |
Domain	No. of HIBs	Mortality	Morbidity	Well-being	Nutrition	Behaviour	Environment	NCDs	Reproductive	NCDs	Mental Health	Eye	HIV	Screening	Inputs	Outputs	Total Health Indicators	Non-Health Indicators
Health																		
Control of Infectious Diseases	1	-	1	-	-	-	-	-	-	-	-	-	1	-	-	-	2	-
Mental Health	8	-	6	-	-	1	-	-	-	-	-	-	-	-	1	7	15	3
Physical Health	17	-	-	7	1	-	-	2	-	3	-	1	-	2	5	12	33	5
Reproductive Health	6	-	4	1	1	2	-	-	3	-	-	-	-	-	1	5	17	1
Sanitation	1	-	-	-	-	-	1	-	-	-	-	-	-	-	-	-	1	-
Substance Misuse	2	-	-	-	-	1	-	-	-	-	-	-	-	-	-	2	3	2
Sub-Total	*35*	*0*	*11*	*8*	*2*	*4*	*1*	*2*	*3*	*3*	*0*	*1*	*1*	*2*	*7*	*26*	*71*	*11*
Non-Health																		
Carers	1	-	-	1	-	-	-	-	-	-	-	-	-	-	-	-	1	1
Criminal Justice	1	-	-	-	-	1	-	-	-	-	-	-	-	-	-	-	1	1
Education	2	-	-	1	-	-	-	-	-	-	-	-	-	-	-	1	2	1
Housing	14	-	-	9	-	-	-	-	-	-	11	-	-	-	-	33	53	14
Unemployment	1	-	-	1	-	-	-	-	-	-	-	-	-	-	1	-	2	1
Young People	4	-	-	4	-	1	-	-	-	-	-	-	-	-	-	1	6	4
Sub-Total	*23*	*0*	*0*	*16*	*0*	*2*	*0*	*0*	*0*	*0*	*11*	*0*	*0*	*0*	*1*	*35*	*65*	*22*
Total	**58**	**0**	**11**	**24**	**2**	**6**	**1**	**2**	**3**	**3**	**11**	**1**	**1**	**2**	**8**	**61**	**136**	**33**

HIB=Health impact bonds.

Table 5.5 Level of intervention

Domain		Prevention							Healthcare				
		Primordial or Primary		Primary	Secondary		Tertiary	Total	Primary Care		Secondary Care		Total
		Fiscal	Regulation	Education, Communication and Information	Preventive Treatment	Screening	Rehabilitation or Ongoing Treatment		GPs	Community Services	Hospitals	Clinics	
Health	Control of Infectious Diseases	-	-	-	-	1	1	2	-	1	-	-	1
	Mental Health	-	-	-	-	-	7	7	-	8	-	-	8
	Physical Health	-	-	6	1	2	8	17	-	10	1	1	12
	Reproductive Health	-	-	4	2	-	-	6	-	3	-	3	6
	Sanitation	-	-	1	-	-	-	1	-	-	-	-	0
	Substance Misuse	-	-	-	-	-	2	2	-	1	-	1	2
	Sub-Total	0	0	11	3	3	18	35	0	23	1	5	29
Non-Health	Carers	-	-	-	1	-	1	2	-	-	-	-	0
	Criminal Justice	-	-	-	-	-	1	1	-	-	-	-	0
	Education	-	-	-	1	-	1	2	-	-	-	-	0
	Housing	-	-	1	1	-	13	15	-	-	-	-	0
	Unemployment	-	-	-	-	-	1	1	-	-	-	-	0
	Young People	-	-	3	1	-	2	6	-	-	-	-	0
	Sub-Total	0	0	4	4	-	19	27	0	-	-	-	0
	Total	0	0	15	7	3	37	62	0	23	1	5	29

Health domain

Within the health domain, the 35 impact bonds follow a similar coverage pattern to health impact bonds in general (see Table 5.2). All 17 countries contain at least one health domain impact bond, only four countries contain >2 (UK (11); USA (6); Japan (3); and Russia (3)) and over 70% of these are located in high-income countries.

There are six sub-domains: control of infectious diseases; mental health; physical health; reproductive health; sanitation; substance misuse (see Table 5.3). Only three sub-domains contain >2 impact bonds: physical health (17); mental health (8) and reproductive health (6). Online Appendix Table 5.1 details the specific focus of the interventions. For example, interventions in physical health focused on cataract surgeries, hypertension, cancer screening, diabetes, physical disabilities, asthma, blood banks and end-of-life care. Boxes 5.2 and 5.3 describe a physical health and reproductive health impact bond, respectively. Table 5.2 shows that three sub-domains are found in high-income countries only (control of infectious diseases; mental health and substance misuse), one sub-domain is in a middle-income country only (sanitation) and two sub-domains are found in high-, middle- and low-income countries (physical health and reproductive health). All seven DIBs are in the health domain

---

Box 5.2   Hachioji City SIB on increasing the rate of residents receiving bowel cancer screenings

The 'Hachioji City SIB' is an impact bond in the physical health domain that aims to increase the rate of bowel cancer screening among residents in Hachioji City, Japan. The funded intervention acts at the level of secondary prevention screening.

Launched in 2017, the outcome payer is Hachioji City. A service provider, Cancer Scan, uses artificial intelligence to analyse the medical information of residents who have not been screened for bowel cancer in the previous fiscal year. Personalised messages are then sent via postcards to encourage screening uptake. 8.87 million Japanese Yen was raised from investors, the Social Impact Investment Foundation, Digisearch and Advertising, and Mizuho Bank. Three health indicators trigger payments: detection of early cancer (health status-morbidity); cancer screening (service coverage-screening); and precision examinations (health systems-output). There are no non-health indicators. Tokyo Institute of Technology, Cancer Scan and University of Tokyo are the evaluators and the intermediary is k-three.

---

and categorised in three sub-domains (see Online Appendix Table 5.1): reproductive health (4); physical health (2); and sanitation (1).

Three impact bonds in the health domain feature health status indicators only; 13 have health status indicators with a combination of other health indicator(s) and/or non-health indicator(s); six have other health indicator(s) and non-health indicator(s); and 13 had other health indicator(s) only (see Table 5.3). Just over half (71) of all health indicators are from impact bonds in the health domain; only 11 of these impact bonds contain non-health indicators (see Table 5.4). Similar to health impact bonds in general, the ordering, by frequency, of health indicator categories is: health systems (33), health status (19), service coverage (10) and risk factors (9). Only two types of health indicator are used >10 times: health systems-outputs (26) and health status-morbidity (11). There are no service coverage-mental health indicators.

Six impact bonds fund interventions that are prevention only, two are healthcare only and 27 are a combination of prevention and healthcare (see Table 5.3). All but one of the prevention only interventions is in physical health; the other is sanitation. The two

---

Box 5.3   Cameroon Kangaroo Mother Care (KMC) DIB

The Cameroon KMC DIB is an impact bond in the reproductive health domain that aims to provide KMC in selected hospitals in Cameroon and integrate KMC into Cameroon's public healthcare system. The funded intervention acts at the level of secondary prevention-preventive treatment and primary care-community services.

Launched in 2018, the outcome payer is Cameroon's Ministry of Public Health and Nutrition International. The service provider is the Kangaroo Foundation who provides KMC in ten hospitals across five regions in Cameroon. KMC is a health practice aimed at low birth weight or preterm newborns. It involves mothers or caregivers providing skin-to-skin contact with their baby, feeding them breastmilk, minimising time in hospital and when mother/baby return home following up with them. $800k was raised from Grand Challenges Canada (the investor). Two health indicators trigger payments: improvements in weight gain for low birth weight or premature newborns (risk factors-nutrition) and increase in access to quality KMC (health systems-output). There are no non-health indicators. The intermediaries are Social Finance UK and MaRS Center for Impact Investing. The evaluator is undisclosed.

healthcare only interventions are in mental and physical health, respectively (see Table 5.1). Again, like health impact bonds in general, the two most frequent levels of intervention are tertiary prevention-rehabilitation or ongoing treatment followed by primary prevention-education, communication and information (see Table 5.5). Within healthcare, the vast majority of impact bonds are primary care-community services. Twenty-six impact bonds target high-risk groups and nine are population-wide (see Table 5.3).

Non-health domain

Within the non-health domain, the 23 domain impact bonds are found over a much narrower range of countries (see Table 5.2). Only three countries have at least one non-health domain impact bond: UK (18); Australia (4); and USA (1). All of these impact bonds are in high-income countries and none are DIBs (see Online Appendix Table 5.1).

Again, there are six sub-domains: carers; criminal justice; education; housing; unemployment; young people (see Table 5.3). Only two sub-domains contained >2 impact bonds: housing (14) and young people (4). Box 5.4 describes an impact bond in housing.

No impact bonds have health status only indicators; 16 have health status indicators with a combination of other health indicator(s) and/ or non-health indicator(s); six have other health indicator(s) and non-health indicator(s); and one has other health indicator(s) only (see Table 5.3). Just less than half (65) of all health indicators are from non-health domain impact bonds and all but one of these impact bonds contain non-health indicators (see Table 5.4). The only impact bond without a non-health indicator is in education – Living Learning (see Online Appendix Table 5.1). This impact bond contained one payable indicator related to acute health service use (health systems output) which aimed to act as a proxy for improvements in health, justice, educational and life outcomes. The ordering by frequency of health indicator categories is also similar in the non-health domain: health systems (36), health status (16), service coverage (11) and risk factors (2) (see Table 5.4). However, there is a much narrower range of health indicators: health status-wellbeing; risk factor-behaviour; service coverage-mental health; health systems-input; and health systems-output. Three of these indicators are used >10 times: health systems-output (35); health status-wellbeing (16); and, service coverage-mental health (11).

All 23 interventions that are in the non-health domain are prevention only (see Table 5.5). There are only three levels of prevention: tertiary prevention-rehabilitation or ongoing treatment (19); primary prevention-education, communication and information (4); and secondary prevention-preventive treatment (4). All impact bonds target high-risk groups (see Table 5.3).

Box 5.4   Entrenched Rough Sleeping SIB – Greater Manchester

The Entrenched Rough Sleeping SIB is an impact bond in the housing domain that aims to provide permanent supportive housing with personalised and flexible support to entrenched rough sleepers in Greater Manchester, UK. The funded intervention acts at the level of tertiary prevention-rehabilitation or ongoing treatment.

Launched in 2017, the outcome payer is Greater Manchester Combined Authority and the Ministry of Housing, Communities and Local Government. It is one of seven Entrenched Rough Sleeping SIBs that operate in different locations in England. It was supported with funds from the UK's Department for Communities and Local Government, Rough Sleeping Programme. There are four service providers: GM Homes Partnership; Great Places; Shelter; and The Brick. The programme uses a housing first approach to assist the most entrenched rough sleepers (people over the past two years who regularly sleep rough and/or are well-known to homelessness services) find secure accommodation. Wrap-around services provide intensive emotional and practical support and help individuals access health, training and employment services that suit their needs. £1.8 million was raised from One Manchester, Trafford Housing Trust and a group of organisations sourced through Bridges Fund Management. Seven health indicators trigger payments: Warwick Edinburgh Wellbeing Scale (health status-wellbeing); mental health entry into engagement with services (service coverage-mental health); mental health sustained engagement with services (service coverage-mental health); alcohol entry into engagement with structured treatment (health systems-output); alcohol sustained engagement with structured treatment (health systems-output); drug misuse entry into engagement with structured treatment (health systems-output); and, drug misuse sustained engagement with structured treatment (health systems-output). A number of non-health indicators also trigger payments around, for example, entering and sustaining accommodation. The intermediary and evaluator are undisclosed.

Discussion

Through our mapping exercise, we identify 58 health impact bonds and categorise these by level of intervention, delivery mechanisms, policy domain, target population and health indicators. This provides an unprecedented insight into the nature and reach of health impact bonds in the health system. In what follows, we use our conceptual framework to discuss whether health impact bonds have untapped potential or represent a broken promise and if they target the source, or effects, of the problem.

Untapped potential or a broken promise?

It is fair to say that, although impressive, the rate of growth of health impact bonds, since the first was implemented in 2011, indicates that like many other health reform claims over the years their transformative promise has not yet been fulfilled.

A key selling point of impact bonds is the claim that they focus on outcomes (11,49). This is supposed to encourage innovation in service delivery and helps differentiate them from more traditional contracts where payments are based on inputs or outputs. However, our mapping exercise raises questions about the nature of health impact bonds as few focus explicitly on achieving outcomes.

In our mapping exercise, we define outcomes as health status indicators; those concerned with impacts on mortality, morbidity and well-being. Given that Iovan et al. (36) find all impact bonds have the potential to impact on health and well-being through the social determinants of health we could expect that most, if not all, of the 225 impact bonds now operating would feature health status indicators. However, this is not the case. Only three health impact bonds, all in the health domain, utilise health status indicators only to trigger payments. Given the focus on outcomes only we could think of these as archetypal impact bonds. A second group, featuring half of the health impact bonds (n=29) retain a focus on outcomes but also utilise inputs, processes and/ or outputs to trigger payments (i.e. risk factors, service coverage, health systems) and/or non-health indicator(s). However, 26 impact bonds do not include any health outcome indicators. Of these, 12 feature non-health indicator(s) alongside other health indicator(s). It is possible that these non-health indicator(s) are outcome indicators in other domains, such as housing or criminal justice; categorising these indicators was beyond the scope of our mapping exercise. Nevertheless, almost 25% of all health impact bonds (n=14) make no payments based on outcomes. It is unclear how these figures relate to impact bonds in general; as far as we are aware no other study has focused on this issue.

We can also look at this by examining the usage of different types of indicators across all health impact bonds. The most common indicator is health systems-output; around 45% of all indicators. While only approximately 25% of all indicators are some type of health outcome indicator (i.e. mortality, morbidity, well-being). Again, this highlights that the activities of an intervention rather than the impact of the intervention trigger payments.

There are two ways of looking at these results. First, health impact bonds are missing a trick by not including health outcome indicators. Just because health outcomes are not measured does not mean impact has not occurred. Thus, there might be untapped potential for investors to receive payments based on inclusion of health outcome indicators. This is important, given the large scope for growth of impact bonds in a number of countries throughout the world, particularly in middle- and low-income countries and in particular domains such as reproductive health and sanitation. Alternatively, these findings suggest impact bonds are failing to live up to their promise. Failing to focus on outcomes undermines one of the key rationales for impact bonds. It is unclear why this is the case but we propose two possible, related, reasons. First, if outcomes are hard to define this could, partially, explain why bonds are not transformative. Second, outcomes measured through, for example, randomised controlled trials, are really a statistical concept that are good at evaluating 'on average' how well a policy is working; typically, we learn little about how and why an effect has occurred. Thus, using such outcomes deterministically to trigger financial payments is likely to run into difficulties. Whatever the reason for not focusing on outcomes the fact that this occurs raises questions about abilities to assess the outcomes, and impact on health system efficiency, of such bonds as an overall policy initiative and, thus, the receipt of further financial and political support.

Focusing on the source, or the effects, of the problem?

Another persuasive narrative that exists around impact bonds is that they focus on preventive activities (10,11,34,35). An often-used analogy around targeting complex social problems is that policies and interventions should aim to tackle issues at their source, or further upstream, rather than responding to problems by focusing on modifying behaviours once they have emerged downstream; this analogy has been used to describe interventions that act on health since the 1970s (50). A similar argument exists for interventions funded via impact bonds, which by focusing on preventive interventions should, in theory, result in savings to government from improved outcomes. However, despite claims that impact bonds focus on preventive issues, it is not clear *how* preventive impact bonds are. Through our mapping exercise, we highlight that health impact bonds, in general, act further downstream.

We find no primordial prevention interventions funded via health impact bonds and no primary prevention-fiscal or -regulation interventions. The most upstream level of prevention identified is primary-education, communication and information while the most frequently found level of prevention is tertiary-rehabilitation or ongoing treatment. This means that most impact bonds fund interventions concerned with reducing the effects of an issue that is already ongoing rather than trying to inhibit the development of the issue in the first place. This is emphasised by the finding that within the health domain, a significant number of interventions operate at the level of primary care. Therefore, while there is evidence of impact bonds funding preventive activities, it appears that these interventions are not targeted at the source of the problem. Failure to do so also raises a question about the sustainability of outcomes beyond the life of the impact bond, which could be at risk once the intervention ceases but the problem remains.

In a seminal paper, Geoffrey Rose (46) outlines two potential approaches to prevention: a population and a high-risk approach. The former aims to shift the distribution of a risk factor across the whole population e.g. legislation to reduce salt content in food. While the former, targets only those considered a high-risk of suffering the issue under consideration with a more tailored intervention e.g. medication for reducing blood pressure. When we apply these categories to health impact bonds, we find that only approximately 16% of interventions take a population approach; no intervention in the non-health domain uses this approach.

In applying Rose's two approaches to health impact bonds, our aim is not to judge the appropriateness of each individual impact bond but to point out the advantages and disadvantages of each so they are considered when conceiving of which approach to take. The high-risk approach could result in an intervention tailored to the specific needs of the individual and result in a larger risk reduction for the individual. However, such an approach may only have a temporary effect, be unsustainable over the long term and not tackle the underlying issue. For example, a large number of impact bonds exist in the housing domain that target individuals who sleep rough. While these interventions, in general, offer wrap-around services (e.g. for health, employment, education) in addition to trying to find stable and permanent housing (see the Entrenched Homelessness Social Impact Bonds) they do not target the conditions that lead to homelessness. On the other hand, a population approach is more likely to tackle underlying causes of the specific issue and result in a larger reduction of the risk factor but may not result in large changes at the individual level and would also require substantial societal changes demanding of political will and a public mandate. For example, the Menstrual Health and Hygiene Impact Bond in Ethiopia aims to promote good practices for menstrual health and hygiene amongst all of society. While this should help challenge prevailing social norms, it may not necessarily lead to big changes at the individual level. The key take away is that it need not be an either/or decision; the use of a holistic approach featuring population and high-risk approaches could help maximise health gains. Therefore, the appropriateness of the individual intervention funded via an impact bond needs to be considered in relation to the broader strategy for targeting the specific social problem. Related to what has been discussed in the previous subsection, it may be that, by taking the easier path to measurement and associated financial reward, health impact bonds are currently distorting activity away from addressing the real health needs of societies.

Conclusion

Currently, health impact bonds play a relatively minor role in health systems throughout the world. This could be because, beyond high-income countries, they are still in a nascent phase of development with large scope for growth. Whether this is viewed positively depends, in part, on how innovations that use market forces are viewed in the health system. This will depend on the ideological standpoints of key policy actors, decision-makers and governments. In this chapter, we highlight other key considerations – do impact bonds live up to claims made about them? Through our mapping exercise, we call into question the claim that impact bonds focus on outcomes and fund preventive interventions that seek to deal with problems at their source. As outlined in Chapter 3, given pressures on health budgets, the latter point is not necessarily an issue and impact bonds could conceivably play an important role in health(care) financing. A key question then becomes do health impact bonds offer value for money as compared to alternative financing strategies. However, failing to focus on outcomes is fundamental. It undermines one of the key rationales for impact bonds, makes assessment of their impact on health system efficiency hard to measure, calling into question their continued financial and political support. Whether this issue is prevalent amongst other impact bonds is unknown. Nevertheless, it becomes important to understand why this is the case. Failure to reframe the focus of impact bonds on outcomes could, at worst, bring down the whole project or, at best, result in it going the same way as many claims of transformative health reforms before it; whereby health impact bonds have a place and a level, but not one that will be fundamental to core health(care) funding.

References

1. Nur A, Messere P. *Reconnecting Social Impact Bonds to 'win-win-win' in practice*. The Government Outcomes Lab. 2022.
2. Disley E, Rubin J, Scraggs E, Burrowes N, Culley D, Europe R. *Lessons learned from the planning and early implementation of the Social Impact Bond at HMP Peterborough*. London: Ministry of Justice; 2011 p. 86.
3. Gustafsson-Wright E, Bogglid-Jones I, Nwabunnia O, Osborne S. *Social and development impact bonds by the numbers*. Brookings Institution; 2022. (Global Impact Bond Database).
4. Liebman J, Sellman A. *Social Impact Bonds: A Guide for State and Local Governments*. Harvard Kennedy School. Social Impact Bond Technical Assistance Lab; 2013.
5. Cabinet Office. *Open Public Services White Paper*. London: Cabinet Office; 2011.
6. Broccardo E, Mazzuca M, Frigotto ML. Social impact bonds: The evolution of research and a review of the academic literature. *Corp Soc Responsib Environ Manag.* 2020;27(3):1316–1332.
7. Carè R, De Lisa R. Social Impact Bonds for a sustainable welfare state: The role of enabling factors. *Sustainability.* 2019;21;11(10):2884.
8. Lantz PM, Rosenbaum S, Ku L, Iovan S. Pay for success and population health: Early results from eleven projects reveal challenges and promise. *Health Affairs.* 2016;35(11):2053–2061.
9. Warner ME. Private finance for public goods: social impact bonds. *Journal of Economic Policy Reform.* 2013;16(4):303–319.
10. Fraser A, Tan S, Lagarde M, Mays N. Narratives of promise, narratives of caution: A review of the literature on Social Impact Bonds. *Social Policy & Administration.* 2018;52(1):4–28.
11. Social Finance. *A Technical Guide to Developing Social Impact Bonds*. London: Social Finance; 2013.
12. Katz AS, Brisbois B, Zerger S, Hwang SW. Social Impact Bonds as a funding method for health and social programs: Potential areas of concern. *American Journal of Public Health.* 2018;108(2):210–215.
13. Sinclair S, McHugh N, Huckfield L, Roy MJ, Donaldson C. Social Impact Bonds: Shifting the boundaries of citizenship. 2014;14.
14. Schinckus C. Financial innovation as a potential force for a positive social change: The challenging future of social impact bonds. *Research in International Business and Finance.* 2017;39:727–736.
15. Tan S, Fraser A, McHugh N, Warner M. Widening perspectives on social impact bonds. *Journal of Economic Policy Reform.* 2019;1–10.
16. Oroxom R. Structuring and Funding Development Impact Bonds for Health: Nine Lessons from Cameroon and Beyond. 2018;41.
17. Centre for Global Development, Social Finance. Investing in Social Outcomes: Development Impact Bonds. *The Report of the Development Impact Bond Working Group*. Centre for Global Development & Social Finance; 2013.
18. Sinclair S, McHugh N, Roy MJ. Social innovation, financialisation and commodification: a critique of social impact bonds. *Journal of Economic Policy Reform.* 2019;1–17.

19. Fox C, Albertson K. Is payment by results the most efficient way to address the challenges faced by the criminal justice sector? *Probation Journal*. 2012;59(4): 355–373.

20. McHugh N, Sinclair S, Roy M, Huckfield L, Donaldson C. Social impact bonds: a wolf in sheep's clothing? J Poverty *Soc Justice*. 2013;21(3):247–257.

21. Carter E. More than marketised? Exploring the governance and account-ability mechanisms at play in Social Impact Bonds. *Journal of Economic Policy Reform*. 2021;24(1):78–94.

22. Edmiston D, Nicholls A. Social Impact Bonds: The role of private capital in outcome-based commissioning. *J Soc Pol*. 2018;47(1):57–76.

23. Roy MJ, McHugh N, Sinclair S. Social Impact Bonds – Evidence-based policy or Ideology? 2017;16.

24. Tan S, Fraser A, Giacomantonio C, Kruithof K, Sim M, Lagarde M, et al. An evaluation of Social Impact Bonds in Health and Social Care. 2015;92.

25. Lowe T. Debate: The cost of SIBs. *Public Money & Management*. 2020;40(3): 185–188.

26. Alenda-Demoutiez J. A fictitious commodification of local development through development impact bonds? *Journal of Urban Affairs*. 2020;42(6): 892–906.

27. Gruyter E de, Petrie D, Black N, Gharghori P. Attracting investors for public health programmes with Social Impact Bonds. *Public Money & Management*. 2020;40(3):225–236.

28. Albertson K, Bailey C, Fox J, LaBarbera C, O'Leary C, Painter G. *Payment by Results and Social Impact Bonds: Outcome-Based Payment Systems in the UK and US*. Bristol: Policy Press; 2018.

29. Joy M, Shields J. Austerity in the making: reconfiguring social policy through social impact bonds. *Policy Polit*. 2018;46(4):681–695.

30. Galloway I. Using Pay-for-success to increase investment in the nonmedical determinants of health. *Health Affairs*. 2014;33(11):1897–1904.

31. Morely J. Dream of Social Impact Bonds should not blind us to their dangers. *Policy Innovation Research Unit*; 2017.

32. Joy M, Shields J. Social Impact Bonds: The next phase of third sector mar-ketization? *Canadian Journal of Nonprofit and Social Economy Research*. 2013;4(2):39–55.

33. Tse AE, Warner ME. The razor's edge: Social impact bonds and the fi-nancialization of early childhood services. *Journal of Urban Affairs*. 2020; 42(6):816–832.

34. Rowe R, Stephenson N. Speculating on health: public health meets finance in 'health impact bonds.' *Sociology of Health & Illness*. 2016;38(8):1203–1216.

35. Hulse ESG, Atun R, McPake B, Lee JT. Use of social impact bonds in fi-nancing health systems responses to non-communicable diseases: scoping review. *BMJ Glob Health*. 2021;6(3):e004127.

36. Iovan S, Lantz PM, Shapiro S. "Pay for success" projects: Financing inter-ventions that address social determinants of health in 20 countries. *Am J Public Health*. 2018;108(11):1473–1477.

37. Government Outcomes Lab. Government Outcomes Lab. *Impact Bond Dataset*. 2022.

38. WHO. *Saving Lives, Spending Less: A Strategic Response to Noncommunicable Diseases*. Switzerland, Geneva: World Health Organization; 2018.

39. Iovan S, Lantz PM. Social Impact Bonds: A promising public-private partnership model for public health. *American Journal of Public Health*. 2018; 108(8):e6–e6.

40. Jain A. *Five Ways for Social Impact Bonds to Live up to Their Potential*. World Bank Blog. 2019.

41. WHO. *Health policy*. World Health Organisation; 2022.

42. WHO. *2018 Global Reference List of 100 Core Health Indicators (Plus Health-Related SDGs)*. Geneva: World Health Organization; 2018.

43. Thomson K, Hillier-Brown F, Todd A, McNamara C, Huijts T, Bambra C. The effects of public health policies on health inequalities in high-income countries: an umbrella review. *BMC Public Health*. 2018;18(1):869.

44. Porta M. Prevention. In: *A Dictionary of Epidemiology [Internet]*. Oxford University Press; 2016.

45. Saltman RB, Rico A, Boerman WGW. Primary care in the driver's seat? Organizational reform in European primary care. *European Observatory on Health Systems and Policies*; 2006, p. 250–252. (European Observatory on Health Systems and Policies Series).

46. Rose G. Sick individuals and sick populations. *International Journal of Epidemiology*. 1985;14:32–38.

47. The Brookings Institution. Outcomes-based financing: Impact bonds and outcomes funds. 2022.

48. Social Finance. Impact Bond Global Database. 2022.

49. Government Outcomes Lab. *Impact bonds*. The Government Outcomes Lab. 2022.

50. McKinlay JB. A Case For Refocusing Upstream: The Political Economy Of Illness. In: *Patients, Physicians, and Illness: A Sourcebook in Behavioral Science and Health*. New York, NY: Free Press; 1979. p. 9–25.

6 Social finance ... *acting on* health

Introduction

What links the joint recipients of the 2006 Nobel Peace Prize – the Grameen Bank and its founder Muhammad Yunus – and the recipients of the 2019 Nobel Memorial Prize in Economic Sciences – Esther Duflo, Abhijit Banerjee and Michael Kremer? The answer – microcredit. Microcredit refers to the provision of small loans at affordable interest rates to individuals who cannot access mainstream lenders due to a lack of collateral and/or credit history. The former received their award for creating bottom-up economic and social development through the provision of this product and the latter for undertaking experimental research on approaches to alleviate global poverty, including microcredit. By any stretch of the imagination, microcredit is a global phenomenon. Microfinance finance institutions (MFIs) managed a total Gross Loan Portfolio of $187.3 billion worldwide and serve an increasing number of borrowers that reached 156.1 million in 2021 (1). The success of MFIs reaching financially excluded individuals is through the development of innovative lending and repayment mechanisms to overcome financial market failures (see Chapter 2) that lead to the exclusion of the worse-off in society from mainstream financial institutions. In this way, the 'unbankable' is transformed into the 'bankable poor' (2). However, microcredit is also a divisive topic. Some view it as a neoliberal response to poverty while others conceive of it as an alternative economic form and the utilisation of randomised controlled trials (RCTs) has cast doubt on its transformative effect.

Microcredit is typically viewed as a financial development tool to facilitate self-employment through business loans or consumption smoothing through personal loans. However, this atypical form of lending is also conceived as having the potential to act as a stimulant to the determinants of health (see Chapter 4). Linking microcredit (and microfinance) to health is not new. However, this work generally focuses on the more instrumental, direct relationship; for example, using

DOI: 10.4324/9781003305248-9

microcredit to purchase health services or offering microinsurance or microsavings products for health (this is the focus of Chapter 7). A nascent area of interest is the relationship between microcredit (itself) and health and well-being. Indeed, this is how we all came together to work in the Yunus Centre at Glasgow Caledonian University from 2010 onwards; our aim, then as well as now, was to conceptualise and evidence microcredit as a non-obvious, community-based public health initiative. We saw this as important due to the need to assess the potential of such approaches in light of persistent and widening health inequalities in Scotland and elsewhere.

In this chapter, we will first introduce microcredit, discussing the innovations that led to its rapid worldwide development and outlining debates around its provision and impact. We then turn to the relationship between microcredit and health. We outline theory on mechanisms through which microcredit might impact health outcomes and present evidence from low-, middle- and high-income countries with respect to such relationships.

What is microcredit?

Microcredit involves the provision of very small loans to individuals who lack collateral and/or credit history and subsequently are often excluded from mainstream financial institutions (3). While predominately associated with low- and middle-income countries, forms of MFIs also operate in high-income countries of, for example, Europe and North America (see Box 6.1 for a discussion of Grameen America and Grameen in the UK). Microcredit is usually provided via MFIs. MFIs take a variety of diverse institutional forms, ranging on a spectrum from non-profit Non-Government Organisations and credit cooperatives with social missions to for-profit non-bank financial institutions and even formal, regulated commercial banks.

Box 6.1   Grameen America and Grameen in the UK

Commencing operations in New York City in 2008, Grameen America has now expanded to 24 cities across the United States of America (USA), having disbursed over 800,000 loans worth close to $3 billion. Retention and repayment rates in Grameen America are very strong (93% and 99%, respectively) and the programme has enhanced both savings and incomes of its participants, as well as their credit scores. This has been achieved by strong leadership, the development of partnerships and associated funding and by working with, but also being able to adapt, the basic Grameen model of group work. One major adaptation was a move towards introducing greater use of technology, as opposed to working with cash, in its loan repayment system and other aspects of record keeping.

A recent RCT not only showed enhanced savings and incomes of Grameen study participants relative to controls but also greater feelings of well-being and social connectedness. To further support clients, Grameen developed 'Promotoras,' a health promotion and empowerment programme which, since 2016, has served nearly 18,000 women. Using a community health worker model in non-clinical settings, 'Promotoras' works directly with clients to create individualised health plans, collect biomarkers such as blood pressure levels, make referrals to local providers and help with healthcare system navigation. More information about the trial and the history of Grameen America can be obtained from https://www.grameenamerica.org.

Commencing slightly later, in 2014, and with the initial support of Tesco Bank, Whole Planet Foundation and Moffat Charitable Trust, Grameen in the UK did not meet with the same degree of success and, indeed, ceased operations in 2018. Initially working in Glasgow, the plan was to expand to other communities around Scotland. To some degree, this did in fact happen, and loan targets were exceeded in the early years of its operation. In June 2017, Grameen had provided business loans to over 400 individuals without credit history or collateral. The lending strategy was based on the traditional Grameen five-people group lending model. The groups met weekly with Grameen staff to receive support and make their payments; however, the group culture was never 'bought into' in the same way as in the USA; clients were based further away from each other and meetings were costly in terms of time and money for them. The main type of business was retail and wholesale (60%), followed by creative activities such as jewellery making or sewing clothes (19%) and trades (9%). Each member got an initial business loan of £1,000, and if the income generating activity was successful, they could progress to a larger loan of £2,500 in year 2 and £5,000 in year 3. However, Grameen's business model was ambitious, aiming for financial sustainability in only four years, and this required that clients could afford the repayment of increasing loan sizes and interest rates as well as impeccable repayment rates. Eventually, the scheme ran into cashflow problems with a number of customers having fallen too far into arrears. High default rates may have been related to nearly half of Grameen in the UK clients, unusually for Grameen, being male (42%). Compared to Grameen America, despite generous support, the success story was never achieved to the same extent in the UK.

Microcredit is not a new idea. Precursors to the modern idea of microcredit provision exist in countries throughout the world in the form of, for example, rotating savings and credit associations, accumulating savings and credit associations and other (in)formal forms of lending (see Chapter 2 for further discussion). The institutions behind its modern development are the Grameen Bank and BRAC, both originating from Bangladesh, and ACCION's Recife Programme in Brazil. From the 1970s onward, these institutions led the formalisation and development of lending and repayment mechanisms to circumvent the forms of market failure – adverse selection and moral hazard (see discussion in Chapter 2) – which led, and continue to lead, to the exclusion of the poorest in society from formal capital markets (4,5). These mechanisms, which form the basis of microcredit theory and underpin the success of microcredit in terms of reaching the financially excluded, fall into two main categories: targeting of women borrowers and contract design.

Women borrowers

Microcredit is synonymous with women borrowers. There are two related reasons for this. In some countries, women have traditionally had fewer opportunities, less social mobility and a lower social standing than their male counterparts (6,7). Targeting women is a potential way to challenge unequal gender relationships and societal norms and impact empowerment. However, there is literature disputing some of these claims, with evidence of prevailing gender norms being reinforced when women do not control their loans (8). More pragmatically, in institutions such as the Grameen Bank in the late 1980s and early 1990s, women were targeted because of initial repayment problems associated with male borrowers (9,10). Perversely, women's lack of social mobility and alternative sources of finance led to a greater responsiveness to the features of contract design (outlined as follows) that MFIs implemented to overcome financial market failures and induce repayment (6,11).

Contract design

The four main forms of contract design are as follows: group lending, public repayments, repayment schedules and dynamic incentives.

Group lending

A lending mechanism made famous by microcredit is group lending. One particular form, associated with the Grameen Bank, is group members being jointly liable for each other's loan. Consequently, if one group member defaults, all other members are denied access to future loans. Group lending was developed to counteract the problems of adverse selection and moral hazard and an extensive literature on this form of lending exists (12–14).

Groups tend to be composed of five members and are generally self-selecting. They take advantage of relational ties and group members' informational advantages arising from knowledge of each other. For example, joint liability incentivises individuals to form groups with others who they deem 'safe'; 'risky' individuals are then more likely to form groups with other 'risky' individuals. This reduces lender's risk in two ways. First, self-selection acts as a screening device. Second, cross-subsidisation occurs. This acts as a form of collateral. Safer borrowers are less likely to default, so will only take responsibility for their own loans. On the other hand, 'risky' borrowers are more likely to cross-subsidise each other due to their increased risk of default.

Despite these advantages, joint liability group lending is now less common. For lenders, an unintended consequence of this approach is if one group member defaults, others could purposely default to avoid the costs of joint liability. This would reduce lender's repayment rates. For borrowers, an opportunity cost exists with time, travel and costs associated with regular group meetings. Joint liability can lead to peer monitoring and group pressure that can raise tensions within groups, harming social capital. Loan size can also increase group tension, as group members may be unwilling to bear the costs for members who want to loan progressively higher amounts. Consequently, microcredit lenders now favour individual liability loans. However, groups are still often utilised to retain their social support.

Public repayments

Public repayments occur within groups or within centres formed of different groups from the same MFI. This provides two main benefits (3,15). First, making repayments in front of others heightens social sanctions, incentivising borrowers not to default. Second, it reduces lenders' transaction costs as repayments and the issuance of new loans occurs in the same place. This is of particular benefit for rural lending in poorer communities where the lender has to go to the borrowers.

Repayment schedules

Microcredit lending generally utilises frequent (i.e. weekly or fortnightly repayments) and regular repayment schedules starting almost immediately after loan issuance. There are three main advantages to this approach (16–18). First, early and frequent contact with borrowers provides lenders with an early warning system to detect, and intervene to help, struggling borrowers. Second, it can instill repayment discipline in borrowers. Third, as making small, regular repayments resembles saving strategies, learning this skill could benefit borrowers in the future. However, this repayment mechanism could also raise problems.

Immediate and frequent repayment, even in small amounts, requires borrowers to have money available to make repayments. While a potential issue with all types of loans, it could be particularly problematic for business loans. The increased onus on generating revenues quickly could lead to more short-sighted investments with immediate revenue potential. Repayment pressure could also lead to borrowers seeking multiple loans from different MFIs. This increases the risk of borrowers becoming stuck in a vicious cycle of debt; the microcredit crisis in Andhra Pradesh, India, is an example of the possible destructive impact of multiple loans (see 'A neoliberal strategy or an alternative economic space?' section for further discussion).

Dynamic incentives

MFIs utilise dynamic incentives to discourage borrowers from strategically defaulting (3,16). Denying borrowers access to future loans is a negative incentive, while the opportunity to access increasingly larger loan sizes upon successful completion of a loan is a positive incentive. The latter refers to progressive lending and also enables lenders to screen out borrowers failing to make repayments on small loans.

Challenges and debates

Two of the main debates around microcredit are the principles and values underpinning its provision and its impact.

A neoliberal strategy or an alternative economic space?

Contrasting views exist about MFIs providing microloans to financially excluded individuals. One view sees microcredit as a neoliberal strategy while another conceives of it as a potential alternative economic space within a diverse economy.

The first view portrays microcredit as a market-based approach to development that contributes to the spread of neoliberalism (19). This critique is primarily aimed at for-profit MFIs and the provision of microloans for businesses. The thesis centres on this form of lending, propagating economic and social development through self-help and individual entrepreneurship and making profit from doing so to the detriment of other development strategies. For example, supporting the small and medium enterprise sector, which through economies of scale provides more scope for creating jobs and growth enterprises, and/or more community-oriented forms of lending that have the interest of borrowers' front and centre. Giving fuel to this thesis are microcredit crises, such as the one in Andhra Pradesh, and the commercialisation of the sector.

In 2010, a microcredit crisis occurred in the Indian state of Andhra Pradesh where there were suicides among indebted borrowers. This crisis was attributed to a number of factors, including usurious interest rates charged by the MFIs, coercive repayment practices by field officers and unprecedented competition among MFIs in the state that made multiple borrowing commonplace (20). Of particular concern was the lack of adequate regulation that enabled these practices to occur. In response, the Reserve Bank of India implemented regulations for the industry in 2011 and has continued to make regulatory changes, such as the regulatory framework for microcredit loans introduced in 2022, designed to further safeguard borrowers and harmonise the regulatory framework for different forms of MFI lenders. Other microfinance crises have occurred in, for example, Nicaragua, Bosnia and Morocco (21).

The growth of the microfinance sector has led to the commercialisation of some parts of the sector. In 2000, commercial banks as well as international private and public investors started funding MFIs. A small number of MFIs also started raising capital from international equity markets via initial public offerings (IPOs). The most high-profile examples are the IPOs of Compartamos in Mexico and SKS Microfinance in India in 2007 and 2010, respectively. Commercialisation raises ethical questions about profiting from the poor and also leads to concerns about mission drift whereby MFIs focus on financial efficiency rather than serving the poor (22).

The second view starts from the premise that a diverse array of economic practices exist in society. While some practices principally focus on profit maximisation, others are driven by more social values. Gibson-Graham (23) conceptualises this idea as the diverse economy. Within the finance sector of the economy, Gibson-Graham outlines three types of market: the mainstream (e.g. private banks); alternative (e.g. microfinance, community-based financial institutions, credit unions); and non-market (e.g. rotating credit funds). A key question in this conceptualisation is what does 'alternative' mean?

'Alternative' economic spaces can diverge from the mainstream in different ways through, for example, their values, goals and structures (24). In relation to institutions, a helpful conceptualisation is alternative-oppositional; alternative-additional; and alternative-substitute (25). Alternative-oppositional institutions reject the values and identities associated with the mainstream and choose to operate differently. Alternative-additional institutions are competitors to the mainstream and may not have different values. Alternative-substitute institutions aim to fill the gap vacated by the mainstream and do not necessarily try to be an alternative.

While alterity is rarely static, this conceptualisation provides a lens to understand how aspects of microcredit lending differ from mainstream lending. However, it is a relatively underutilised theory in relation to microcredit. The only known empirical study is of microloans for business in the UK (26). These lenders are conceptualised by supply-side stakeholders as alternative-oppositional providers of credit as the needs of (potential) borrowers are embedded within their operating model by an onus on responsible lending through relationship banking practices. This stands in contrast to the characterisation of microcredit as a neoliberal strategy. Importantly, what these polarised views help highlight is that given the size and diversity of the microcredit sector across and within countries in terms of MFI, loan type, mission, lending, repayment and operating model, it is difficult to make general claims about the nature of microcredit provision.

The impact of microcredit: lead or supporting actor?

A lot of the backlash against microcredit stems from claims about its impact. In the 1990s and early 2000s, a common view was that microcredit could alleviate poverty. While suspicions should be raised about any single social intervention claiming to act as a silver bullet, part of the issue around microcredit was that research took time to catch up with the growth of the field. It is important to note that many schemes were started at arms length by the government or the private sector because, initially, neither supported microcredit. Anecdotal evidence, practitioner-led qualitative research and biased quantitative studies dominated the field. Off the back of poverty alleviation claims, critics argue that MFIs received funding that would have been more usefully spent elsewhere. A reaction to concerns about the perceived quality of initial microcredit impact evaluations, particularly in disentangling causation from correlation (27,28), was the utilisation of RCTs.

RCTs are often promoted as the "cleanest way" to evaluate the effectiveness of social and development interventions (29, p. 8). They are claimed as the best way to identify what is responsible for an observed effect (the attribution problem) and for making sure the observed effect is not dependent on characteristics of the borrowers (i.e. selection biases). A number of high-profile microcredit RCTs exist that cast doubt on its transformative effect (27). Instead, in general, modestly positive effects are found across different indicators, such as stabilising income, increasing profits of pre-existing businesses and increasing happiness. Importantly, the impact of microcredit is not the same for all borrowers.

While RCTs have provided useful insights into the effect of microcredit, the emphasis given to this method requires consideration. RCTs are not without critique, and, indeed, new evidence has emerged recently that the RCTs may have underestimated the impact of microcredit (30,31). It could be argued, on one hand, that the naïve adoption of RCTs from medicine as a gold standard failed to account for the context in which such trials are possible in the medical field. For example, much work in medicine goes into assessing the potential for trials to be undertaken in ways that render their results both valid and generalisable. We would contend that this has been problematic in the context of the microcredit trials. Uptake of microcredit has not been as expected in many 'intervention' areas (30). Issues of consent to participation in an experiment are also not clear from many such studies, as are issues of the negative psychological impact of not being permitted access to microcredit and how this has impacted the leakage of study recruits, initially allocated to control groups, into intervention groups. Some of these challenges are related to the lack of equipoise and the restriction of people's rights (to access credit) which then lead to trials being conducted in very particular circumstances (e.g. amongst those who have just missed out on being extended a loan) but severely limit generalisability (32,33). In medical research, most of these issues are dealt with via prior, and often quite extensive, feasibility studies which have never been undertaken for microcredit trials.

Also, by the time trials had been embarked upon, the world of medicine (and the wider health area) had moved on. This is reflected in the UK Medical Research guidelines on *Developing and Evaluating Complex Interventions* (34). These apply particularly to community-based public health initiatives which would share many characteristics with microcredit. Indeed, as will be seen in the following text, in our own work, we have even portrayed microcredit as a public health intervention. Other innovative methods exist, such as financial diaries, that have identified the important role microcredit plays in helping individuals manage their complex financial lives (35,36). This issue is not that other methods will evidence microcredit directly, so alleviating poverty. Rather that failure to recognise the limitations of RCTs will lead to missed impacts and a lack of understanding about how impact occurs. This is of particular importance when we consider the relationship between microcredit and health.

Microcredit and health

As outlined in Chapter 4, there are limits to health(care) policy for reducing health inequalities and a need to identify and evidence other initiatives that could act on the determinants of health. In the rest of this chapter, we make the case for microcredit provision as a non-obvious public health measure. By 'non-obvious' (37,38), we mean that through its general use, and lending and repayment mechanisms, microcredit has the potential to impact upstream determinants of health, even though impacting health is not a stated objective or mission. First, we outline the theoretical case for microcredit acting in this way and then present evidence. In doing so, we draw on examples from low-, middle- and high-income countries.

Theory

Two main theoretical contributions exist that link microcredit and health (33,39).

In the first theoretical contribution, Mohindra and Haddad (39) construct a framework that links female microcredit participation with determinants, and pathways, of population health, health production theory and Sen's capability approach (see Figure 6.1). Four potential pathways – economic, social, psychosocial and political – are outlined, with corresponding mechanisms, as outputs of female participation in microcredit. Through the economic pathway, female borrowers gain increased, or improved access, to economic resources, collective resources or public goods and services and improve their overall material conditions. The social pathway works through the provision of social support, changing social norms and attitudes and increasing women's social engagement and social participation. The psychological pathway operates through an increase in a woman's self-efficacy and the development of a woman's sense of coherence. The final pathway is the development of a greater political 'voice.' The production or conversion channels convert these mechanisms into proximate determinants of health. The former channel maintains, protects or restores health by acting as inputs into health production, while the latter channel converts existing or available health

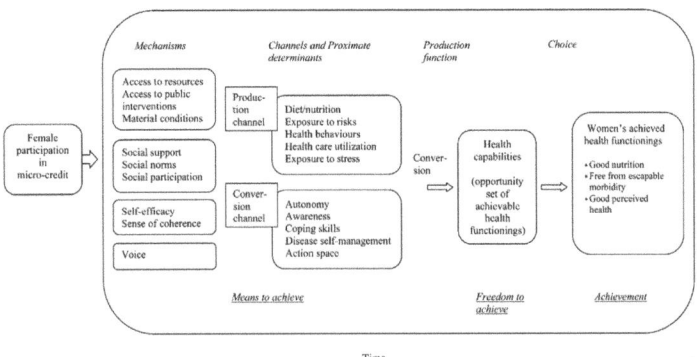

Figure 6.1 Microcredit participation and women's health[1].

inputs into good health. The ultimate outcome of this process is an individual's opportunity to achieve good health (i.e. health capability) and actual health states (i.e. health functionings).

The second theoretical contribution portrays the potential relationship between microcredit and health and well-being as a complex intervention, utilising a social determinants of health lens (33) – see Figure 6.2. The starting point for this theory is that prospective clients are likely to be among the most materially worse-off in society, suffer from financial exclusion and potentially unemployment (26,40,41). Thus, they are more likely to be suffering from poorer health and well-being as health and mental health inequalities in the UK follow a social gradient, and wealth, income and power are recognised as important determinants of these inequalities (42–45). In line with a social determinants approach, the potential relationship between microcredit and health is shown at three levels – individual, community and society – and four classifications of mediating mechanisms are delineated. These are as follows: 1) individual characteristics, 2) engagement with microcredit, 3) health behaviours and health investments and 4) individual assets.

Thus, from both models, it is proposed that this atypical form of lending has the potential to act as a non-obvious public health measure by impacting psychosocial and physical aspects of health (33). It is important to recognise, however, that access to microcredit, by nature, involves becoming indebted and there is a wide literature suggesting indebtedness contributes to the development of mental and physical health problems, see, for example, Sweet et al. (46). Similarly, while self-employment (a potential outcome of microcredit for enterprise) has long been associated with greater autonomy and control over decision-making, studies also show self-employed individuals are considered to be more susceptible to isolation and job stress and, for some, this could be a precarious form of employment (47–51). Moreover, the complex pathways through which impact is likely to occur mean that it is unlikely to act in the same direction; for example, transitioning from unemployment to self-employment may improve self-esteem and feelings of purposefulness if employment is meaningful but not improve income levels and could reduce the time available for family life or socialising.

The potential for adverse impacts, along with the establishment of conceptual frameworks, provides strong reasons as well as a framework for evaluating 'microcredit as a public health initiative.' Given their recent prominence, seeking to examine microcredit in this way takes us back to considering the results from the recent RCTs, but, alongside that, equal consideration of even-more-recent observational studies as well as innovative mixed-methods designs using financial diaries and qualitative methods. This leads us to an interesting juncture in assessing the evidence base for microcredit providing public health benefits, which,

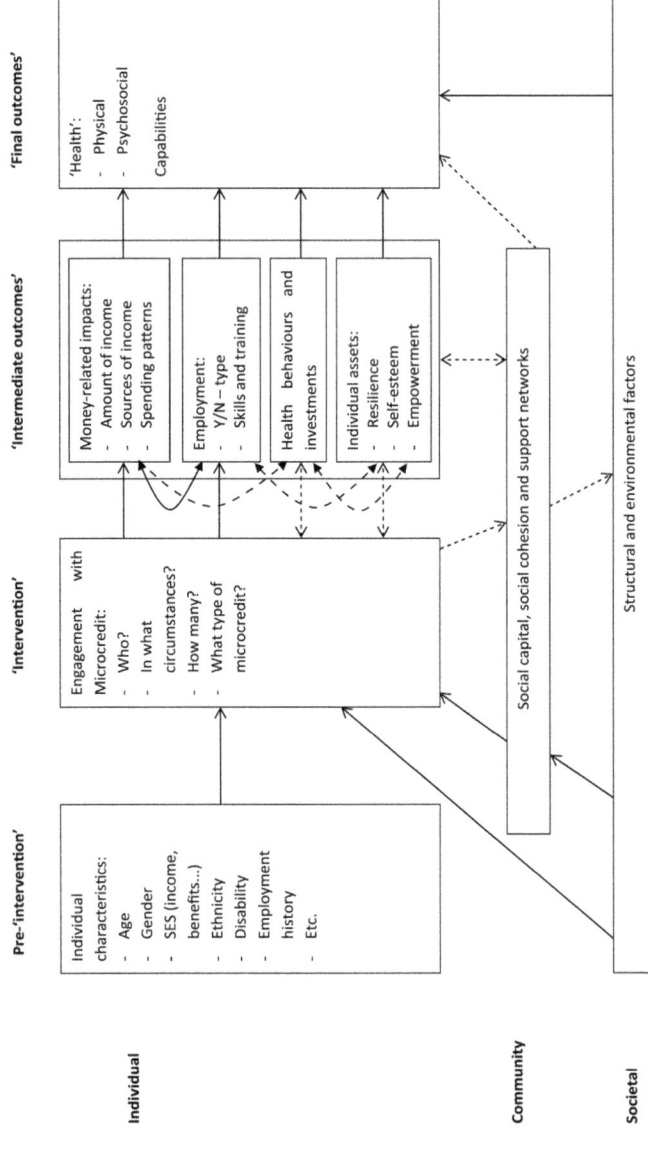

Figure 6.2 Microcredit, health and well-being[2].

beyond market failure arguments, might further strengthen its case for support from the government.

Evidence

Empirical academic evidence of the link between microcredit, by itself, and health, in its broadest sense, is growing but still scarce. Traditionally, the literature has been focused on better understanding the relationship between microcredit programmes which include a health component, for example, HIV prevention, and specific health outcomes linked to that particular health component. This body of literature, while also relevant and the focus of our next chapter, focuses on microcredit programmes that have been specifically designed to facilitate access to health(care). In this chapter, we are particularly interested in the evidence linking small loans, in and of themselves, to health outcomes.

Ironically, one of the first papers that assessed the direct connection between access to microloans and health and well-being outcomes was an RCT conducted with South-African microcredit borrowers (52). Mixed effects were found on the borrowers' mental health. While access to credit increased perceived psychological stress, it was also associated with reduced depressive symptoms in men, but not women. The authors offer plausible explanations for these results, stressing the need for including health outcomes when assessing the impact of microcredit programmes. It was following their lead that one of the only other RCTs directly connecting microcredit and health was published. This RCT assessed the impact of microloans offered by the well-known Mexican MFI Compartamos Banco through 16,560 surveys of potential borrowers (53). The authors included the more traditional domains for the evaluation of microcredit – income, microentrepreneurship, labour supply, expenditures and social status – and added subjective well-being measures including depression, stress, locus of control, life and financial satisfaction and health status. In general, the study finds no transformative effects across any of these outcomes, positive or negative. It does, however, find reductions in the depression index (which was designed specifically for this study and is not standard in the health economics literature). Both of these studies are subject to the aforementioned limitations but find interesting connections that deserve further exploration.

Alongside these RCTs, there were two cross-sectional studies systematically linking microcredit and health. The pioneering study connecting microcredit *per se* and health was conducted in Bangladesh with BRAC clients. While no differences in emotional stress were found between microcredit users and non-users, borrowers reported less depression symptoms but more fatalistic/resigned attitudes (54). In the second study, conducted in South India, findings suggested lower levels of self-reported emotional stress for those who had borrowed from the MFI for at least two years (55).

While income is the main pathway through which microcredit impacts health, there is evidence of other social determinants of health, such as social connectedness or women empowerment, that mediate this effect (52,56). There is a large body of literature that explores these mediating mechanisms, though not necessarily including health measures as such. In what is, to our knowledge, the only systematic review exploring the impact of microloans without 'plus' programmes on health and social outcomes, Gichuru et al. (57) highlight the need for more evidence as results are mixed. In particular, the authors select contraceptive use, female empowerment (intimate partner violence, decision-making ability and mobility) and children's nutrition as outcomes of interest and include RCTs, cross-sectional and panel data analyses in South Asia, Sub-Saharan Africa and Latin America and the Caribbean (n=27). Interestingly, they did not include any observational studies, even if these were screened. They found that microcredit borrowers were significantly more likely to report contraceptive use, mixed results for the association between microloans and intimate partner violence and some positive changes in female empowerment and children's nutrition. However, the wide diversity of reported outcomes, study design, statistical methods, contexts and microcredit supply models did not allow for any causal claims. The authors argue for more rigorous research, such as RCTs. We, however, have argued and continue to do so that it is precisely this diversity and complexity that require the use of alternative research designs to understand in-depth the connection between microcredit and health and well-being (33).

Since 2014, we have explored the association between people's financial lives (including the use of microcredit and other community-based initiatives) and their health and well-being in the UK. Through different research projects, all part of the FinWell programme of work, we have explored different mechanisms and mediators of the finance and health relationship (microcredit access, long-term health conditions, COVID-19 pandemic and Cost of Living crisis). All FinWell projects take a mixed-method approach using financial diaries and longitudinal in-depth interviews.

The success of the 'financial diaries' as a method to reveal the intertemporal complexities of financial management for people with low and middle incomes was shown in 'Portfolios of the Poor' (35) and, later, in the US Financial Diaries (58). In combination with monthly in-depth qualitative interviews, recording and analysing daily financial transactions (incomings and outgoings) over time provides a detailed insight into the financial lives of individuals and households as well as the accompanying rationales underlying their decision-making. As a methodological innovation to explore the connection between microcredit and health, we incorporated 'health diaries' into this approach. These include standardised patient-reported outcome measures such as SF12v2 and ICECAP, as well as keeping a detailed record of the health events of participants. These are, for example, medical visits, diagnosis, treatment and hospitalisation. We also record respondents' subjective perceptions of the relationship between microcredit initiatives and other community-based programmes and their own and their community's health and well-being. An example of how this connection is evidenced is portrayed by Daliya's case study presented in Box 6.2. Daliya was one of the participants of our FinWell London Financial Diaries study, funded by the UK charity Impact on Urban Health, and the project team met with her from July to December 2019 (59).

Box 6.2   Microcredit and health in the UK: Daliya's case

Who is Daliya?

Daliya is 27 years old and from the UK. She has two children under six years old and they live in London. After her children were born, Daliya had to stop working full-time because her salary was not enough to cover childcare costs. Daliya is partially sighted from birth and has suffered from mental health issues. When we meet her, Daliya is looking for a part-time job and finishing a degree in computing and mathematics.

Why does she experience big changes in income?

Daliya is receiving a UK welfare benefit called Disability Living Allowance to help her with mobility or care costs due to her vision problem. In July 2019, this benefit was stopped, without warning, to be replaced by a different one called Personal Independent Payment. Welfare payments were not resumed until October 2019.

How does she manage?

At first, Daliya relies on her savings, which quickly ran out. She then takes three loans from two microcredit providers (Fair Finance and Oakam) – one per month from July to September. With no income at all, taking out loans was the only way in which her family could survive.

How does the connection between microcredit and health look like for Daliya?

When Daliya's welfare benefits are stopped, the score of her Mental Health Composite Scale (SF12v2) also drops. When she accesses microcredit, her mental health improves proportionally. Finally, when her welfare benefits kick in again, her mental health goes back to the level prior to the income drop. Benefits were paid retrospectively which enables Daliya to pay back her microloans. Income and mental health remain inversely correlated throughout the six months of financial diaries. The graph, as shown in Figure 6.3, illustrates the relationship between Daliya's income and mental health (as measured by the SF12v2).

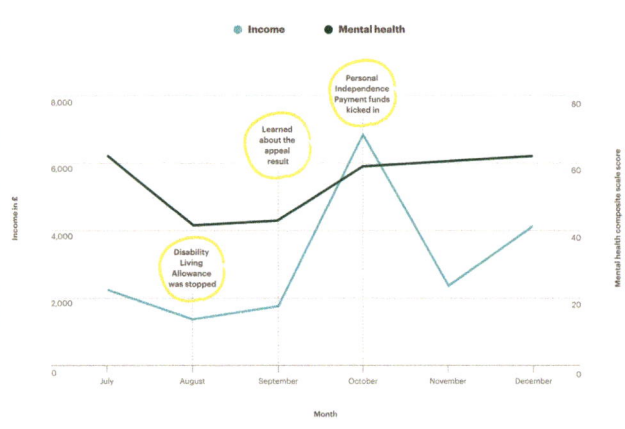

Figure 6.3   Daliya's income and mental health from July to December 2019[3].

Source: Guy's & St Thomas' Foundation (60).

Across the different FinWell projects, we have consistently found that microcredit is being used as a coping strategy that protects borrowers from drops in income and expenditure shocks. The financial resilience that responsibly delivered microcredit can provide is positively associated with the health and well-being of borrowers (36,56). In our Glasgow FinWell study, microcredit, and the mechanisms through which it was delivered by two local providers (Scotcash and Grameen in the UK), were perceived by participants as positively impacting their health and well-being. It reduced stress, helped preserve social relationships and empowered borrowers to gain control over their own lives. In some cases, receiving the loan also caused stress, which is frequently linked to lending model features such as group lending schemes (56). These results were corroborated in our FinWell London study, where microcredit provided financial security and contributed to better health scores. However, our London participants were found to be managing simultaneously several forms of formal and informal credit. This involved making financial decisions extremely frequently. These decisions are hard for low-income groups because of their urgency, serious implications and, sometimes, being impossible to reverse. Consequently, they increase stress levels, absorbing mental 'bandwidth' to the detriment of other important aspects of participants' lives (36).

In the aftermath of COVID-19, the increasing academic interest in testing a theory of change for microcredit that includes a health and well-being dimension has met with the industry's need to provide accurate and reliable outcome measures for impact investors. This is enlarging the body of secondary data that considers the impact of microfinance on health in its broadest sense. Pioneer industry-wide initiatives have started to include in their data intelligence health-related outcomes both at MFI and client-level. For example, the 60 Decibels Microfinance Index, which collects comparable data on the impact of microfinance on over 4,400 borrowers in 15 countries, includes dimensions such as nutrition, quality of life and healthcare spending. This information has allowed lead organisations in the sector to better portray their impact. For instance, Symbiotics, the market access platform for impact investing, states in its impact report that, in 2021, microfinance had 'very much improved' the quality of life of 35% of the borrowers in their portfolio, 'very much increased' household spending on healthcare for 9% and 'very much increased' the number of quality meals for 14% of microfinance borrowers in their portfolio (61). These results can now also be compared to impact averages of the sector as a whole, enabling the identification of investors and asset managers with higher social impacts. These datasets can also be used for more academic research around the connection between microcredit and health.

Conclusion

Exploring the relationship between microcredit (itself) and health and well-being is a nascent area of research. Yet, despite the relative paucity of work, there are promising signs of microcredit acting as a socio-economic determinant of health within low- and high-income countries. Importantly, there is no one-size-fits-all approach. Diverse microcredit practices will affect individuals in different ways, leading to different impacts on health and well-being. As outlined, this has implications for the evaluation approach utilised, with a need to break from the (now) RCT orthodoxy. While it is unlikely that microcredit will significantly reduce entrenched health inequalities, given the size of the market, it has the potential to impact positively on the health of millions of vulnerable people and, therefore, be part of the solution. If realised, microcredit could be a standard-bearer for non-obvious ways to impact health and, particularly in contexts where provision is jeopardised by issues of sustainability, increase its claim for greater public policy support.

Notes

1 Women's Interlaced Freedoms: A Framework Linking Microcredit Participation and Health, Katherine S. Mohindra and Slim Haddad, Journal of Human Development and Capabilities, 2005, volume 6, issue 3, pages 353–374, Taylor & Francis Ltd, reprinted by permission of the publisher (Taylor & Francis Ltd, http://www.tandfonline.com).' to 'Women's Interlaced Freedoms: A Framework Linking Microcredit Participation and Health, Katherine S. Mohindra and Slim Haddad, Journal of Human Development and Capabilities, 2005, Taylor & Francis Ltd, reprinted by permission of the publisher (Taylor & Francis Ltd, http://www.tandfonline.com).
2 Neil McHugh, Olga Biosca, and Cam Donaldson, Evaluation: The International Journal of Theory, Research and Practice, volume 23, issue 2, pages 209–225, copyright © 2017 by (Copyright Holder), reprinted by permission of SAGE Publications.
3 Reprinted from 'Daliya's story', *FinWell: London Financial Diaries,* image created by Soapbox Communications Limited, copyright © 2021 by Guy's & St Thomas' Foundation.

References

1. Convergences. *Impact Finance Barometer 2022.* Convergences: Zero Exclusion Carbon Poverty; 2022.
2. Weber H. The "new economy" and social risk: Banking on the poor? *Review of International Political Economy.* 2004;11(2):356–386.
3. Armendariz B, Morduch J. *The Economics of Microfinance.* MIT Press; 2010.
4. Hermes N, Lensink R. The empirics of microfinance: What do we know? *The Economic Journal.* 2007;117(517):F1–F10.
5. Roodman D. *Due Diligence: An Impertinent Inquiry into Microfinance.* Center for Global Development; 2012.
6. Rahman A. Micro-credit initiatives for equitable and sustainable development: Who pays? *World Development.* 1999;27(1):67–82.
7. Schuler SR, Hashemi SM, Badal SH. Men's violence against women in rural Bangladesh: Undermined or exacerbated by microcredit programmes? *Development in Practice.* 1998;8(2):148–157.
8. Kabeer N. Conflicts over credit: Re-evaluating the empowerment potential of loans to women in rural Bangladesh. *World Development.* 2001;29(1):63–84.

9. Khandker SR, Khalily B, Khan Z. *Grameen Bank: Performance and Sustainability.* Washington: World Bank; 1995.

10. Todd H. *Women at the Center: Grameen Borrowers after One Decade.* New York: Routledge; 1996.

11. Goetz AM, Gupta RS. Who takes the credit? Gender, power, and control over loan use in rural credit programs in Bangladesh. *World Development.* 1996;24(1):45–63.

12. Ghatak M. Screening by the company you keep: Joint liability lending and the peer selection effect. *The Economic Journal.* 2000;110(465):601–631.

13. Stiglitz JE. Peer monitoring and credit markets. *The World Bank Economic Review.* 1990;3(4):351–366.

14. Armendariz B, Gollier C. Peer group formation in an adverse selection model. *The Economic Journal.* 2000;110(465):632–643.

15. Besley T, Coate S. Group lending, repayment incentives and social collateral. *Journal of Development Economics.* 1995;46:1–18.

16. Armendáriz B, Morduch J. Microfinance beyond group lending. *Economics of Transition.* 2000;8(2):401–420.

17. Rutherford S. *The Poor and Their Money.* New Delhi: Oxford University Press; 2000.

18. Morduch J. The microfinance promise. *Journal of Economic Literature.* 1999;37(4):1569–1614.

19. Bateman M. *Why Doesn't Microfinance Work?: The Destructive Rise of Local Neoliberalism.* London: Zed Books Ltd; 2010.

20. Mader P. Rise and fall of microfinance in India: The Andhra Pradesh crisis in perspective. *Strat Change.* 2013;22(1–2):47–66.

21. Bateman M, Chang HJ. Microfinance and the Illusion of Development: From Hubris to Nemesis in Thirty Years. 2012;1.

22. Hudon M, Sandberg J. The ethical crisis in microfinance. *Business Ethics Quarterly.* 2013;23:561–589.

23. Gibson-Graham JK. Rethinking the economy with thick description and weak theory. *Current Anthropology.* 2014;55(S9):S147–S153.

24. Leyshon A, Burton D, Knights D, Alferoff C, Signoretta P. Towards an ecology of retail financial services: Understanding the persistence of door-to-door credit and insurance providers. *Environment and Planning A: Economy and Space.* 2004;36(4):625–645.

25. Fuller D, Jonas A. Alternative Financial Spaces. In: *Alternative Economic Spaces.* London: SAGE Pubications; 2003. pp. 55–74.

26. McHugh N, Baker R, Donaldson C. Microcredit for enterprise in the UK as an 'alternative' economic space. *Geoforum.* 2019;100:80–88.

27. Banerjee A, Karlan D, Zinman J. Six randomized evaluations of microcredit: Introduction and further steps. *American Economic Journal: Applied Economics.* 2015;7(1):1–21.

28. Roodman D, Morduch J. The impact of microcredit on the poor in Bangladesh: Revisiting the evidence. *The Journal of Development Studies.* 2014 April 3;50(4):583–604.

29. Banerjee A, Duflo E. *Poor Economics: A Radical Rethinking of the Way to Fight Global Poverty.* New York: Public Affairs; 2011.

30. Dahal M, Fiala N. What do we know about the impact of microfinance? The problems of statistical power and precision. *World Development*. 2020;128: 104773.

31. Breza E, Kinnan C. Measuring the equilibrium impacts of credit: Evidence from the Indian microfinance crisis. *The Quarterly Journal of Economics*. 2021;136(3):1447–1497.

32. Abramowicz M, Szafarz A. Ethics of Randomized Controlled Trials: Should Economists Care about Equipoise? In: *Randomized Control Trials in the Field of Development: A Critical Perspective*. Oxford University Press; 2020. pp. 280–292.

33. McHugh N, Biosca O, Donaldson C. From wealth to health: Evaluating microfinance as a complex intervention. *Evaluation*. 2017;23(2):209–225.

34. Skivington K, Matthews L, Simpson SA, Craig P, Baird J, Blazeby JM, et al. A new framework for developing and evaluating complex interventions: Update of Medical Research Council guidance. *BMJ*. 2021;374:n2061.

35. Collins D, Morduch J, Rutherford S, Ruthven O. *Portfolios of the Poor: How the World's Poor Live on $2 a Day*. Princeton University Press; 2009.

36. Biosca O, McHugh N, Ibrahim F, Baker R, Laxton T, Donaldson C. Walking a tightrope: Using financial diaries to investigate day-to-day financial decisions and the social safety net of the financially excluded. *The ANNALS of the American Academy of Political and Social Science*. 2020;689(1):46–64.

37. Macaulay B, Roy MJ, Donaldson C, Teasdale S, Kay A. Conceptualizing the health and well-being impacts of social enterprise: A UK-based study. *Health Promotion International*. 2017.

38. Roy MJ, Baker R, Kerr S. Conceptualising the public health role of actors operating outside of formal health systems: The case of social enterprise. *Social Science & Medicine*. 2017;172:144–152.

39. Mohindra KS, Haddad S. Women's interlaced freedoms: A framework linking microcredit participation and health*. *Journal of Human Development*. 2005;6(3):353–374.

40. Lenton P, Mosley P. *Financial Exclusion and the Poverty Trap: Overcoming Deprivation in the Inner City*. London and New York: Routledge; 2012.

41. McHugh N, Gillespie M, Loew J, Donaldson C. First steps towards self-employment – Microcredit for enterprise in Scotland. *Scottish Affairs*. 2014;23(2):169–191.

42. Macintyre A, Ferris D, Gonçalves B, Quinn N. What has economics got to do with it? The impact of socioeconomic factors on mental health and the case for collective action. *Palgrave Communications*. 2018;4(1):10.

43. Marmot M. Fair Society: Healthy Lives. *Strategic Review of Health Inequalities in England Post-2010*. (The Marmot Review).

44. Jones AM, Wildman J. Health, income and relative deprivation: Evidence from the BHPS. *Journal of Health Economics*. 2008;27(2):308–324.

45. Wilkinson RD, Pickett K. *The Spirit Level: Why More Equal Societies almost Always Do Better*. Allen Lane/Penguin Group: Bloomsbury Publishing; 2009.

46. Sweet E, Nandi A, Adam EK, McDade TW. The high price of debt: Household financial debt and its impact on mental and physical health. *Social Science & Medicine*. 2013;91:94–100.

47. Jamal M. Job stress, satisfaction, and mental health: An empirical examination of self-employed and non-self-employed Canadians. *Journal of Small Business Management.* 1997;35(4):48–57.

48. Parslow RA, Jorm AF, Christensen H, Rodgers B, Strazdins L, D'Souza RM. The associations between work stress and mental health: A comparison of organizationally employed and self-employed workers. *Work & Stress.* 2004;18(3):231–244.

49. Lewin-Epstein N, Yuchtman-Yaar E. Health risks of self-employment. *Work and Occupations.* 1991;18:291–312.

50. Benach J, Benavides FG, Platt S, Diez-Roux A, Muntaner C. The health-damaging potential of new types of flexible employment: A challenge for public health researchers. *American Journal of Public Health.* 2000;90(8): 1316–1317.

51. Facey ME, Eakin JM. Contingent work and ill-health: Conceptualizing the links. *Social Theory & Health.* 2010;8:326–349.

52. Fernald LC, Hamad R, Karlan D, Ozer EJ, Zinman J. Small individual loans and mental health: A randomized controlled trial among South African adults. *BMC Public Health.* 2008;8(1):409.

53. Angelucci M, Karlan D, Zinman J. Microcredit impacts: Evidence from a randomized microcredit program placement experiment by Compartamos Banco. *American Economic Journal: Applied Economics.* 7(1):151–182.

54. Ahmed SM, Chowdhury M, Bhuiya A. Micro-credit and emotional well-being: Experience of poor rural women from Matlab, Bangladesh. *World Development.* 2001;29(11):1957–1966.

55. Mohindra K, Haddad S, Narayana D. Can microcredit help improve the health of poor women? Some findings from a cross-sectional study in Kerala, India. *International Journal for Equity in Health.* 2008;7:2.

56. Ibrahim F, McHugh N, Biosca O, Baker R, Laxton T, Donaldson C. Microcredit as a public health initiative? Exploring mechanisms and pathways to health and wellbeing. *Social Science & Medicine.* 2021;270:113633.

57. Gichuru W, Ojha S, Smith S, Smyth AR, Szatkowski L. Is microfinance associated with changes in women's well-being and children's nutrition? A systematic review and meta-analysis. *BMJ Open.* 2019;9(1):e023658.

58. Morduch J, Schneider R. *The Financial Diaries: How American Families Cope in a World of Uncertainty.* NJ: Princeton University Press; 2017.

59. Biosca O, Baker R, Donaldson C, McHugh N, Morgan A, Bala A, et al. *Managing Finances and Multiple Long-Term Conditions: Eliciting the Perspectives of Individuals Living on Low Incomes.* Impact on Urban Health; 2021. p. 106.

60. Guy's & St Thomas' Foundation. *Daliya's Story (FinWell: London Financial Diaries).* Impact on Urban Health; 2021.

61. Symbiotics. *Symbiotics Impact Report 2021.* Tameo Impact Fund Solutions; 2022.

7 Social finance ... facilitating *access* to health(care) services

Introduction

Today, microfinance institutions (MFIs) all over the world offer a variety of financial products to individuals who lack access to mainstream banking services. Their fundamental mission is, in general, to promote financial inclusion. However, the original MFIs, those dating from the 1970s, frequently offered small loans to low-income people as a means to an end that was not solely financial inclusion. Microcredit could be intended, for example, to promote peace and post-conflict reconstruction through community economic initiatives, to empower women and improve livelihoods by encouraging productive activities or to alleviate hunger by increasing agricultural produce. The missions of these first MFIs were holistic and geared towards improving the livelihoods and living conditions of vulnerable communities more broadly rather than being exclusively about income insecurity. Those early lenders soon noticed that borrowers needed to be healthy if they were to make the most of their microloans. Hygiene and maternal and child health education programmes quickly complemented the provision of microcredit. Thus, the direct connection between microcredit and health(care) is evident from the development of modern microcredit.

In Chapter 6, we outlined how particular forms of social finance, such as microcredit, have the potential to transform health and reduce health inequalities by impacting the social determinants of health. In other words, microcredit can be considered a public health intervention. In this chapter, we describe how microfinance can improve access to health (care) services and explain MFIs' rationales for formally facilitating it. We will outline the programmes' evolution and the different health-related financial and non-financial products currently offered by MFIs. We will also present an overview of the academic literature on the causal pathways between these programmes and borrowers' health outcomes.

DOI: 10.4324/9781003305248-10

Finally, we will summarise the main innovations triggered by the COVID-19 pandemic.

Microfinance and health(care)

Microfinance comprises banking services provided to unemployed or low-income individuals or groups who otherwise would have no other access to financial products. Microfinance consists of a broadly defined set of financial services including microcredit, microdeposits and microinsurance products. Microfinance packages can include different types of non-financial services, also known as 'microfinance-plus.' These are supplementary services seeking to enhance the intersectional impact of financial services and to protect microfinance clients more effectively against the negative consequences of exposure to the market (1). There are different types of non-financial services, ranging from those with a social objective – such as education, healthcare and mentoring – to those oriented to improve business performance – such as business training, market linkages and technical assistance – or those focused on environmental outcomes. MFIs with social missions such as ProMujer, Finca International, BRAC and Grameen Bank have been implementing successful integrated programmes where credit is linked to education and other non-financial services for the past few decades (2).

How the microfinance–health connection developed?

The strong link between poverty and ill health is no secret (3–5). As discussed in Chapter 3, access to healthcare is far from equal, particularly in lower-income countries where microfinance originated. For the most vulnerable, the main challenge beyond accessing quality health (care) services is the ability to pay for highly prevalent user charges. With little capacity to invest public funds in effective health systems, an important share of health expenditures in lower- and middle-income countries comes from out-of-pocket sources. Until Universal Health Coverage becomes a reality, estimates indicate that catastrophic out-of-pocket expenditure pushes about 100 million people per year into extreme poverty (6).

Microfinance providers witness first-hand the effects of the two-fold challenges experienced by lower-income groups when seeking health treatments: access and cost. Health shocks are one of the main causes of loan default, either because they might prevent an income earner from working or because money is diverted to pay for treatment. Many health problems are also unpredictable so the situation is aggravated by further difficulties for borrowers in managing income and expenditure variability. Even if microfinance clients end up accessing and paying for healthcare and recovering from their illnesses, the financial consequences of the health shock can be devastating and difficult to surmount. This is particularly the case if clients adopt risky coping strategies such as becoming overindebted or selling productive assets. Some MFIs are aware that they are not only in a position to help with the need to smooth, or finance, their client's health expenditure, but also to support them by reducing the lack of information and cultural barriers that can prevent them from accessing high-quality treatments.

In the early days of microfinance, many MFIs offered, alongside loans, additional health-related services mainly focused on personal and food hygiene practices and antenatal, maternal and child health. These basic health education programmes, of variable quality, were frequently compulsory for the clients and mostly focused on prevention. The rationale for offering plus-health packages was two-fold. Firstly, it was a way for MFIs – mostly NGOs at the time – to fulfil their social, holistic and intersectional missions. Secondly, they were delivered to raise the productivity of the loans and buffer their clients from sudden and severe health shocks. However, by the 1990s, microcredit had attracted the attention of important players in the field of development such as the World Bank. They admired its potential to become a financially self-sufficient tool with the capacity of multiplying the development impact of the donors' funds and investments. Concessional funds were funnelled into MFIs on the condition that there was total specialisation on financial products, as this was considered the only way to achieve the scale required to operate without the need for subsidies or, even, at a profit. This focus on financial sustainability contributed to the discredit, and consequent disappearance, of many credit-plus programmes, including those with a health focus (7).

With the arrival of the 21st century and the global agenda addressing the overlapping vulnerabilities of poverty, social exclusion and health through the Millennium Development Goals (MDGs), the role of microfinance as a platform for health started to be reappraised. It was recognised that access to finance would only improve livelihoods if other dimensions of deprivation were also addressed (8). The microcredit crises (see Chapter 6) also brought to the fore the importance of 'protectional' microfinance packages that prevented the shift in risk from the MFIs to the borrowers and instead helped clients cushion for shocks more effectively (9). These packages became more sophisticated including emergency microloans, savings products, microinsurance and non-financial services, and many of them had a health focus. MFIs started offering these health-related products to help clients: (a) better cope with health emergencies; (b) gain access to affordable preventive health(care) programmes and medical treatments if and when needed; and (c) benefit from health(care) education and promotion (10).

Driven by the international development agenda, MFIs gradually started developing more sophisticated intersectional microfinance programmes. These were designed to ensure that clients were reaping all the possible benefits from microfinance. At the same time, offering these types of packages, which included, for example, access to primary healthcare facilities, also presented institutional advantages in terms of improved management of reputational risk, making the programme more attractive to prospective clients (2) and improving repayment and retention rates (11–13).

During the last decade, this move towards the reconciliation of microfinance and health services was further encouraged structurally by the Agenda 2030 and the need to meet collaboratively the Sustainable Development Goals, established in 2015, but also more organically by the 2013–2016 epidemic of Ebola virus disease centred in Western Africa and the COVID-19 pandemic. These events have stimulated innovation, collaboration and excellence in the integrated microfinance and health arena.

How do integrated microfinance and health programmes work in practice?

At an organisational level, however, offering linked microfinance and health programmes has traditionally presented some challenges. The more general ones are associated with increased managerial complexity and higher operational costs for MFIs which lower their financial sustainability and raise ethical and data protection concerns. These challenges, however, depend on the programme design and type of delivery. The potential types of delivery of health-related microfinance products are outlined in Table 7.1.

In the last few decades, many providers of health-related packages have evolved from a unified mode of delivery, frequently compulsory for clients, to working in partnership with insurance companies, commercial banks, health agencies, healthcare providers and pharmaceutical suppliers, among others. This helped improve the cost-effectiveness of integrated programmes, minimise their impact on the financial viability of the MFIs, reduce managerial complexity and improve the health-related programmes' quality. It is for these reasons that collaborative partnerships are becoming one of the most popular types of delivery (15).

This shift towards creating partnerships has been accelerated worldwide during the COVID-19 pandemic, where, for example, in many countries, governmental agencies have partnered with MFIs for

Table 7.1 Main types of delivery of health-related microfinance products

Types of delivery	Definition	Main products of this type
Unified	The same staff in the same department of the MFI offer both financial and health-related services.	Health emergency loans, health microinsurance, health promotion, etc.
Parallel	Different organisational units of the same MFI deliver the services.	Health education, health promotion, preventive health(care) services, etc.
Partnership	The MFI partners with a public or private health-related organisation to offer health (care) services. Partnerships can be collaborative or cooperative.	Non-financial services that facilitate access to a primary clinic, a local hospital or a pharmaceutical provider.
a Cooperative	The MFI receives support from a health provider to deliver the service. They remain separate entities with independent decision-making, staff and budgets.	Development of training curriculums for health education, training of trainers, linking with national health programmes, referrals to external healthcare providers and organising health camps in MFI areas.
b Collaborative	The MFI and health organisation share decision-making and resources, assume particular roles and responsibilities, are accountable to each other and do not operate independently.	Integrated teaching curricula and health education/promotion programmes, access to health products, access to water and sewer network connections, access to filtered water and bundled health insurance products.

Source: Adapted from Sievers and Vanderberg (14) and Ruducha and Jadhav (15).

vaccination campaigns to leverage their capacity for large-scale and rapid community mobilisation. An example of this is the public–private partnership established between the Indian Government and Equitas Small Finance Bank to reach remote and vulnerable communities in the COVID-19 vaccination campaign. In many other cases during the pandemic, deeply trusted credit officers have ended up switching roles to frontline community health workers.

How popular are integrated microfinance and health programmes?

Integrated programmes have gained popularity and more examples can be found worldwide as well as replications of the most successful programmes in a range of settings. Empirical academic studies on integrated programmes, as well as reviews on their impact, are also gradually increasing. However, these programmes are impossible to quantify. Annual data from the MIX Market database (16) suggest that around 20% of reporting MFIs were offering some type of non-financial service from 2014 to 2019 but the programmes and their duration were not always described. Sometimes there was no information on their type (business, health, social, agricultural and environmental).

A number of MFIs and international development players have traditionally offered and continue offering health packages alongside microcredit. These exemplary MFIs and organisations usually share three characteristics. First, these MFIs originated with, and preserve, strong social missions which make them strong advocates for holistic and intersectional programmes. Secondly, they have a presence in more than one country and frequently operate as networks. This enables these MFIs to be excellent innovators, sharing with each other the results of their pilot programmes and their operational knowledge and expertise for better replication and escalation of integrated programmes. Finally, group lending is their main credit model (see Chapter 6). This provides operational advantages making programme delivery more cost-efficient in unified or parallel models. Group lending also provides a bigger platform for health partners, increasing economies of scope. Table 7.2 outlines some of the pioneer-integrated microfinance and health programmes worldwide.

The growing and current popularity of integrated microcredit and health programmes was recently evidenced by the submissions to the 2021 European Microfinance Award on 'Inclusive Finance and Health Care.' An important number of financial organisations applied for the award in the midst of the pandemic, showcasing a diverse range of healthcare initiatives provided by different types of MFIs in all regions of the world (18).

The role of microfinance in health(care)

Microcredit borrowers have three fundamental barriers to using health-related services, particularly in lower-income countries. The first challenge is the availability of high-quality health(care) services and products, the second obstacle is the affordability of these services and treatments and the third barrier is a lack of knowledge or awareness of the need to use these services (10). MFIs have designed a range of health-related financial and non-financial services and products to overcome each of these challenges. The list of health-related services provided by MFIs and how this delivery is operationalised in practice is outlined in Table 7.3.

Table 7.2 Pioneer-integrated microfinance and health programmes worldwide

Organisation	History, geographic locations and programmes
BRAC	Founded in Bangladesh in 1972 as an NGO with a holistic approach to development, BRAC is now a group of organisations including BRAC Banks, social enterprises, hospitals, socially responsible investments and a university. Since 2001 when its internationalisation started, BRAC Microfinance has grown to become one of the world's largest providers of financial services with a presence in 13 countries in Asia, Africa and Latin America. BRAC has traditionally combined credit services with health and education. They were an early example of partnering with the national government for large-scale health campaigns focused on communicable diseases such as tuberculosis and malaria.
Grameen Bank	Grameen Bank, arguably the first MFI, was founded in Bangladesh in 1976. In 2006, it was awarded the Nobel Peace Prize in appreciation of its efforts to create economic and social development from the bottom of society through microcredit. Grameen Bank always preserved its holistic approach. An example was one of the first Micro Health Insurance products to provide healthcare to clients, and non-clients, in its health centres. Insurance gave access to reduced medical consultation fees, discounts on medicines and medical tests, hospitalisation and free annual health check-ups and immunisations. Today this programme still runs in Bangladesh as part of Grameen Health Care Services, a social business part of the Grameen group. Grameen has worked in 27 countries.
Freedom from Hunger (now part of Grameen Foundation)	Multinational NGO that started operations in the 1970s focusing on maternal and infant health and nutrition. In the 1980s, they started working with MFIs to develop one of the first integrated microcredit and health and nutrition packages. Since then, they have partnered with MFIs to escalate these products in Africa, Asia and Latin America to reach over 21 million people. They pioneered programmes like the Malaria Initiative delivered through MFIs and the Microfinance and Health Protection initiative which gave clients of their partner MFIs access to health savings plans, low-cost health products, preventive health services, healthcare services, health microinsurance and emergency health loans.
ProMujer	ProMujer was founded in 1990 in Bolivia to give opportunities to women so they could become powerful agents of change. Since the start, they used an integrated approach to micro-lending, also offering access to health and educational services. The MFI offers quality, low-cost preventive health services (mammogram, preventive health screening, birth control, in-person counselling, telemedicine) through their own (mobile) clinics and partner institutions in Argentina, Bolivia, Mexico and Nicaragua.

Sources: Organisations' websites, Hamid et al. (17), Leatherman et al. (10).

Table 7.3 Health-related financial and non-financial microfinance products

Product/Service	Challenge	Delivery type
Financial		
Health and emergency loans	Affordability	Microloans specifically designed and delivered by MFIs to cover medical emergencies. These are frequently provided as top-ups of the current loan with a faster approval process to suit coverage of medical emergencies.
Health deposits and saving accounts	Affordability	Health-focused savings products are offered by some MFIs to their borrowers. These deposits can frequently only be withdrawn to cover medical expenses.
Health microinsurance	Affordability	Health microinsurance is provided by MFIs, almost in every case in partnership with a specialised insurance company.
Non-financial		
Health education and promotion	Lack of knowledge	Health education and promotion programmes are offered to clients by MFIs to create awareness and behaviour change around health promotion practices. These can be offered in unified, parallel or partnership types.
Linkages to health providers	Accessibility	Linkages can be direct when the MFI itself provides health services or indirect when the MFI links clients to other public or private health service providers or independent community health workers. These programmes are complex and frequently require the contribution of specialised partners and public providers.
Access to health products	Accessibility	The MFI, frequently through networks of community health workers and trained microfinance clients, facilitates access to high-quality and affordable health-related products such as nutrition supplements, insecticide-treated bed nets, menstrual pads, antibacterial soap, etc.

Integrated financial products and health

The main financial products offered by MFIs for health-related needs are as follows: credit, savings and insurance.

Health-related microloans are delivered to cover unexpected health shocks and pay for health expenses such as medical treatments, consultations, and surgeries, as well as the purchase of medical equipment, accessories and medicines. While the provision of these specific microloans is not too frequent, most MFIs offer some type of emergency loan that can accomplish similar goals. These emergency loans, provided to borrowers at speed and as a top-up of their traditional microloans, are also an alternative way to cover unexpected medical expenses. The loan size is generally small as the MFIs need to ensure affordability for the borrowers who are already indebted to the institution. So, there are limitations in terms of what type of health(care) needs can be financed through this product.

Secondly, health-related savings products where withdrawal is only possible if it is to finance a health(care) need are becoming progressively popular. Again, the amounts deposited are relatively low because microfinance borrowers generally have limited saving capacity, so these products perform better when the health event is known and there is enough time to build capital regularly (e.g. childbirth) (18).

Finally, health microinsurance is also a financial product offered by MFIs to help borrowers finance health(care) expenses. While adding compulsory life microinsurance to microcredit contracts has become relatively frequent, the operational difficulties and cost of offering health microinsurance have limited the number of MFIs offering it. For microinsurance products, the MFIs need to partner with specialised providers. The design of the insurance contracts needs to be adequate for the microfinance borrowers, simple and affordable. In many cases, the insurance companies cannot supply products such as the ones needed by MFI clients in a financially viable way. Scale is key to the financial sustainability of these services but microinsurance products are still not well understood by MFIs target groups and, when these are optional, adoption is generally low. These are complex financial products and to ensure a certain level of take-up, the MFIs offering them need to deploy additional resources on promotion and education of their client base. Even though its provision is challenging, insurance is likely to be the most appropriate financial product to finance health emergencies and well-designed services built through reliable partnerships have been extremely successful. An example featuring the Moroccan MFI Al Amana, one of the most important and well-known MFIs in the Middle East and North Africa (MENA) region, is provided in Box 7.1.

Box 7.1 Al Amana microfinance (Morocco): An example of health microinsurance

Context

In Morocco, the public health system is inaccessible and unaffordable for more than half of the population (53%), who also, generally, cannot afford private health insurance. Doctors, beds, medication and equipment are also limited. Over half of Al Amana's clients (58%) have to pay health services out-of-pocket and health shocks are an important cause for loan default.

Provider

Leader in its sector and in the MENA region, Al Amana Microfinance counts 2,500 staff committed to manage a network of 616 branches, 640 agents and 86 mobile branches to cover remote rural areas. Founded in 1997, Al Amana Microfinance served 322,000 microentrepreneurs as of December 2021, of whom 42% were women and 48% were in rural areas. Al Amana offers inclusive financial services to microbusinesses including loans, money transfers and microinsurance, as well as non-financial services such as business training and support.

Microinsurance programme

Since 2012, Al Amana has been offering the 'Tayssir al Amana' programme to meet clients' health needs in partnership with the insurer Saham Assistance. This microinsurance product features a simple single-policy coverage for childbirth, serious disease, incapacity, hospitalisation and death-related expenses. The insurance contract has been designed for affordability and simplicity. Borrowers only need to pay 1% of the loan instalment as a premium (less than one pound per month) and they can access fixed coverage of up to £450 including coverage of emergency transport to the hospital. Since 2015, the coverage also includes other household members such as partners and children. Claims can be done over the telephone or in the branch without presenting medical documentation and reimbursement can be directly settled at the MFI's branches. Unlike other microinsurance programmes, Tayssir Al Amana has very high outreach among the MFIs' borrowers. As of 2020, over 250,000 clients and their families were insured with this product (79% of the

MFI's client base) and 11,885 claims were settled, almost half of which were for childbirth, with hospitalisation costs, ambulance transport and funeral expenses also making up significant percentages.

Source: Adapted from Mendelson (18)

Integrated non-financial services and health

Health-related non-financial services are designed to address challenges related to both the lack of health knowledge and awareness and the difficulties experienced by microcredit borrowers in accessing high-quality health(care) services. Health education and promotion services are traditionally the most prevalent type of health component in microfinance programmes worldwide. This is evidenced by widespread impact assessments of these programmes (19). The most frequent delivery type is through trained credit officers or health providers during loan repayment meetings. In the early days of microfinance, education and awareness programmes were usually the only health components and compulsory for clients. Nowadays, they are delivered as part of integrated finance and health packages with multiple components; they are opt-in for clients and sometimes for their families and communities too. Even if additional health components have been gradually added to the mix, education has remained the primary element in many health-related programmes because it has proven crucial to changes in health behaviours and the use of health services. An example of one of these programmes – Fonkoze (in Haiti) – is described in Box 7.2. These programmes are focused on a broad range of outcomes that stretch from reproductive, maternal and child health, to prevention and treatment of communicable diseases such as diarrhoea, HIV, tuberculosis or sexually transmitted diseases and infections (e.g. human papillomaviruses).

An important complement to education and awareness programmes is when MFIs provide linkages and referrals to in-house, public or private, primary or secondary, health providers. The ProMujer network in Latin America is a pioneer not only in offering these kinds of non-financial services but also in evaluating their programmes (20). For example, ProMujer Argentina has a health package called *Beneficio Universal* to offer primary healthcare services directly in its branches (mainly preventive screening), as well as through a group of specialist providers if the clients need further treatment. For them, ProMujer Argentina has developed a regional network of providers who have agreed to provide a range of services for fixed/discounted prices to their clients including pharmacies, laboratories, diagnostic

Box 7.2   Fonkoze (Haiti): Multiple component microfinance–health package

Context

Haiti is the poorest country in the Western Hemisphere and has one of the lowest life expectancies in the world (66 years old; ranked 198 out of 227 countries). In Haiti, rural and low-income groups have very limited access to healthcare, frequently only seeking care and treatment when illnesses reach acute stages. Most Haitians need to pay out-of-pocket for their health(care) related expenses.

Provider

Since 1995, Fonkoze provides holistic financial and non-financial services to remote communities in Haiti. Fonkoze is the largest microfinance organisation in the country, with a team of over 300 loan officers who travel every day to rural and hard-to-reach areas to hold monthly meetings with microcredit groups of approximately 20 clients.

Health-related products and services offered

Since 2014, through its Foundation, Fonkoze offers health-related services to borrowers. The programme, called Boutik Santé, is a social franchising model to facilitate clients' access to over-the-counter health products, education and healthcare services. A Fonkoze team of registered nurses' trains selected clients in rural groups as Community Health Entrepreneurs (CHEs) to conduct basic health screenings (e.g. malnutrition), deliver health education sessions and procure health and hygiene products to sell such as antibacterial soap, pregnancy tests and nutrition supplements. This model also provides a business opportunity for CHEs.

Source: Mendelson (18) and CIA (21)

imaging centres and 11 local government institutions. In the most severe cases, they can also provide preferential bureaucracy-free referrals to the public health system. Other common examples of services that MFIs can facilitate access are as follows: mobile health clinics for primary care in remote areas, trained community health workers, prepaid care programmes, medical campaigns or telemedicine services. Finally, MFIs can also facilitate access to health products such as affordable, quality-controlled generic medications and health products. They frequently do this in partnership with pharmaceutical providers and distribute the products through the MFIs network of trained clients or community health workers. Fonkoze (see Box 7.2) is also an example of this practice. In some cases, the MFI directly provides the products such as, for instance, the BotiCARD pharmacies established by the well-known Centre for Agriculture and Rural Development (CARD) in the Philippines. As of July 2021, CARD pharmacies had served almost 1.5 million clients across 12 branches, providing them not only with much needed quality health products but also free, over-the-counter health advice.

Impact of financial and non-financial health products

Academic literature on the impact of integrated health products on health outcomes is still limited but growing fast, in line with the number of operating programmes. The first pioneer articles appeared in academic journals fairly recently, in the years 2001 and 2002, just after the MDGs were adopted. All of them concurred that microfinance-integrated programmes had effects on the health outcomes of clients. A decade later, Leatherman et al. (10) published the first review of the evidence, featuring 17 articles. The authors argued that MFIs could implement health programmes that increase knowledge, change health-related behaviours and facilitate access to health services. They also called for more rigorous research in this area, which they would also review in an updated study published five years later (19). In this second review, the authors find an additional 19 new studies, most with experimental designs (RCTs). The substantial increase in microfinance and health studies, which doubled in just five years, indicates the increasing popularity of this area.

In this review, Lorenzetti and colleagues (19) are unable to synthesise the studies through a meta-analysis due to the diverse study populations, intervention conditions and outcomes. However, this is advantageous as the review is very comprehensive in terms of including different types of health programmes delivered by MFIs (health education and promotion; health financing and health microinsurance; linkages to health providers; access to health products; and programmes with multiple components) and different types of outcomes. Over half of the papers reviewed (n = 20) were evaluating health education and promotion integrated programmes focused on different areas: HIV and sexually transmitted diseases; air, water and vector-borne diseases such as malaria and diarrhoea; and maternal and child health, nutrition and immunisation. The conclusions of the review are optimistic, as most health interventions are found to have positive results, particularly health education programmes which demonstrate clear positive effects on health knowledge and behaviours. The effect of microfinance combined with other health components was less clear due to the small number and quality of studies. The authors argue for the need to increase intervention periods which will enable measurement of more complex pathways to health status.

With results consistent with Lorenzetti et al. (19), Saha and Annear (22) review 26 papers on the role of membership-based microfinance with associated health programmes in improving health outcomes in South Asia. They conclude that the evidence confirms that integrated programmes can improve the health of microcredit borrowers and identify specific pathways through which these impacts can happen (the social and economic situation of the poor, community health, increased health awareness, healthcare financing and affordable healthcare products and services).

Similarly, Orton et al. (23) found improvements in some health outcomes in their systematic review of the health impacts of group-based microfinance for collective empowerment. However, they highlight the need for studies that cope better with bias and the need to assess negative as well as positive social and health impacts. Kennedy et al. (24) also call for more rigorous studies in their systematic review of income generation interventions, including microfinance and vocational skills training, for HIV prevention. They found inconclusive evidence that microfinance and vocational skills interventions including health-related components were effective at changing HIV-related sexual risk behaviours. Another systematic review of 41 articles on microfinance and women's health (25) equally found that the evidence was not conclusive due to the varied quality and reporting in the identified articles. Finally, the most recent systematic review which is strictly focused on the impact of microfinance on non-communicable diseases (NCDs) health indicators and outcomes (26) concurs with the fact that variations in study designs and reporting in the articles limited the ability to draw strong conclusions. However, the authors argue that microfinance may reduce risk factors, promote health-seeking behaviour and reduce out-of-pocket health and catastrophic health expenditure related to NCDs. Importantly, this is the only review in which one study showed negative outcomes of the use of microfinance on NCDs. This was an association between microfinance and higher waist circumference, BMI and obesity rates.

In general, though there is a need for more and better research, most studies confirm the potential of integrated microfinance–health programmes as a health platform to achieve crucial health outcomes for borrowers such as improved health and health-seeking behaviours, access and usage and a reduction of out-of-pocket catastrophic health expenditure.

Innovation after COVID-19

Like in many other sectors, the COVID-19 pandemic has been an important trigger for innovation in microfinance. The need for adaptation of the health-related programmes that were being offered by MFIs before the pandemic as well as the motivation of the other MFIs to include health services into their remit led to a rethinking of focus, operational strategies, staffing, use of technology and cost-efficiency. During the pandemic, many MFIs 'kept calm and carried on' with their activities while facing severe restrictions on the movement of people and on social gatherings. These restrictions impacted the fundamental pillars of the microfinance group lending model, which is key to microfinance acting as a platform to facilitate health(care) access, particularly in remote and rural communities. To continue their operations, MFIs had to innovate in their working models, activities and processes.

While academic evidence is still scarce, sector practitioners collated successful adaptations of microfinance programmes to the new COVID-19 reality. It is worth mentioning here that for many MFIs, networks and investors, this was not the first epidemic context they had to go through. For example, the BRAC microfinance programmes had even produced a case study highlighting lessons learned during the 2014–2016 Ebola epidemic that mainly took place in West Africa (27). Other MFIs, for example in Mexico, also had to adapt their operations during the 2009 'swine flu' pandemic caused by the H1N1 influenza virus. It is perhaps the scale, severity of restrictions and duration of the COVID-19 pandemic that has allowed for more innovative and potentially long-term/permanent approaches such as the use of telephone and digital platforms to cost-effectively facilitate access to healthcare.

The report of the European Microfinance Award 2021 on 'Inclusive Finance and Health Care' (18) collects many of the most successful and long-lasting innovations in microfinance programmes seeking to improve health outcomes. During this period, MFIs focused on preserving the financial resilience of their clients. Many MFIs operating health insurance or prepaid medicine programmes, for example, Microfund for Women in Jordan, subsidised their clients' premiums during the pandemic. This measure would add to the national debt moratoria imposed in many countries worldwide, for example, India and Pakistan, which meant that MFIs had to grant repayment breaks to their borrowers who had seen their repayment capacities deeply affected by the pandemic. In a context of increased liquidity concerns and uncertainty for MFIs, many of them focused on preserving access to affordable healthcare when it mattered the most (18).

The report also features organisations running health education programmes that quickly adapted them to include COVID-19 prevention and treatment strategies. They focused on translation to indigenous languages and found original ways to disseminate this information. Frequently, cars and vans used by MFIs for debt collection and mobile clinics were used to deliver flyers and play recorded messages on loudspeakers to their clients and communities, particularly those more remote and isolated. Some MFIs such as Avanza Sólido in Mexico could also deliver prevention kits (e.g. masks, gel, thermometers and paracetamol). The most interesting innovations are in the field of how MFIs managed to ensure continuity of access to quality healthcare. This was generally achieved through the use of digital technology and leveraging partnerships, mainly with national governments and local authorities, which enabled MFIs to find creative and cost-effective ways to reach clients. For example, Microfund for Women in Jordan started offering a mobile use-now-pay-later telehealth subscription service to all its clients. Many other MFIs scaled up their existing telephone and online consultation programmes if they had ones (e.g. CARD Bank in the Philippines). Some other organisations such as ProMujer started experimenting with health chatbots using artificial intelligence to preserve access to health programmes (28). At the same time, MFIs also delivered remote basic digital training programmes (mainly on the use of Zoom and WhatsApp but also social media) to ensure that clients had sufficient technological skills to access the healthcare services available.

Contrary to what could have been expected, some MFIs increased proximity to their clients, planning individual medical or community health visits. With credit officers being deprived of their main function during debt moratoria, i.e. collecting repayments, many MFIs gave them the opportunity to be trained as COVID-19 community health workers so as to keep in touch, and preserve trust, with their clients, the MFIs' most important asset. Unexpectedly, credit officers became frontline workers which improved their motivation and mental health and could have been key to preserving pre-COVID repayment rates (27). These operational changes were mostly spontaneous. However, some argue that MFIs could have also innovated the incentive structure, which remained linked to traditional performance indicators such as credit recovery, for credit officers during the pandemic period to respond to a different reality and job requirements. This would have reduced staff stress levels and properly reflected loan officers' efforts (29).

Conclusion

This chapter illustrates the pivotal role integrated microfinance and health programmes can play in facilitating access to health and healthcare for the most vulnerable, cushioning microborrowers from catastrophic out-of-pocket expenditure whilst also providing some relief to increasing pressures in national healthcare budgets. The extent and size of these initiatives have progressively increased in recent years and the pandemic has brought substantial innovation to the design and operation of integrated programmes worldwide. Despite the promising evolution of these integrated microfinance programmes, their impact is still unclear, as is their potential to bring transformative change. Challenges remain ahead as the sector needs to explore better ways of increasing the cost-effectiveness, scalability and replicability of these highly contextualised programmes. Although COVID-19 has opened the eyes of governments in terms of the role that the microfinance sector could play in facilitating service provision, coordination is vital across the public and private financial and health sectors to find types of partnerships that ensure equitable, high-quality, effective and efficient access to health(care). Leveraging the synergies of offering integrated microfinance and health programmes can not only contribute to improved health outcomes for microfinance borrowers but also to broader structural change in economies and health(care) systems.

References

1. Biosca O, Lenton P, Mosley P. Where is the 'plus' in 'credit-plus'? The case of Chiapas, Mexico. *The Journal of Development Studies*. 2014;50(12): 1700–1716.
2. Biosca O, Lenton P, Mosley P. Microfinance non-financial services as a competitive advantage: The Mexican case. *Strategic Change*. 2014;23(7–8):507–516.
3. Marmot M. Fair Society: Healthy Lives. Strategic Review of Health Inequalities in England Post-2010. 2010. (The Marmot Review).
4. Marmot M, Allen J, Boyce T, Goldblatt P, Morrison J. *Health Equity in England: The Marmot Review 10 Years On*. The Health Foundation; 2020.
5. WHO. Closing the gap in a generation: Health equity through action on the social determinants of health. Final report of the Commission on Social Determinants of Health. World Health Organisation. *Commission on Social Determinants of Health*; 2008. p. 253.
6. World Health Organization, World Bank. *Tracking Universal Health Coverage: 2017 Global Monitoring Report*. Geneva: World Health Organization; 2017.
7. Berger M, Goldmark L, Miller Sanabria T, Inter-American Development Bank, editors. *An Inside View of Latin American Microfinance*. Washington: Inter-American Development Bank; 2006. p. 295.
8. Pronyk PM, Hargreaves JR, Morduch J. Microfinance programs and better health prospects for sub-Saharan Africa. *JAMA*. 2007;298(16):1925–1927.
9. Aitken R. The financialization of micro-credit. *Development and Change*. 2013;44(3):473–499.
10. Leatherman S, Metcalfe M, Geissler K, Dunford C. Integrating microfinance and health strategies: Examining the evidence to inform policy and practice. *Health Policy and Planning*. 2012;27(2):85–101.

11. Godquin M. Microfinance repayment performance in Bangladesh: How to improve the allocation of loans by MFIs. *World Development.* 2004;32(11): 1909–1926.

12. Karlan D, Valdivia M. Teaching entrepreneurship: Impact of business training on microfinance clients and institutions. *The Review of Economics and Statistics.* 2011;93(2):510–527.

13. Lensink R, Mersland R, Vu NTH, Zamore S. Do microfinance institutions benefit from integrating financial and nonfinancial services? *Applied Economics.* 2018;50(21):2386–2401.

14. Sievers M, Vandenberg P. Synergies through linkages: Who benefits from linking micro-finance and business development services? *World Development.* 2007;35(8):1341–1358.

15. Ruducha J, Jadhav M. A review of organizational arrangements in micro-finance and health programs. *Journal of Global Health Reports.* 2018;2: e2018024.

16. World Bank. MIX Market | DataBank. 2023.

17. Hamid SA, Roberts J, Mosley P. Can micro health insurance reduce poverty? Evidence from Bangladesh. *Journal of Risk and Insurance.* 2011;78(1):57–82.

18. Mendelson S. *Lessons and Best Practices from the European Microfinance Award 2021 on 'Inclusive Finance & Health Care'.* European Microfinance Platform; 2021.

19. Lorenzetti LMJ, Leatherman S, Flax VL. Evaluating the effect of integrated microfinance and health interventions: An updated review of the evidence. *Health Policy and Planning.* 2017;32(5):732–756.

20. Geissler KH, Leatherman S. Providing primary health care through integrated microfinance and health services in Latin America. *Social Science & Medicine.* 2015;132:30–37.

21. CIA. Haiti - The World Factbook. 2023.

22. Saha S, Annear PL. Overcoming access barriers to health services through membership-based microfinance organizations: A review of evidence from South Asia. *WHO South-East Asia Journal of Public Health.* 2014;3(2): 125–134.

23. Orton L, Pennington A, Nayak S, Sowden A, White M, Whitehead M. Group-based microfinance for collective empowerment: A systematic review of health impacts. *Bulletin of the World Health Organization.* 2016;94(9): 694–704.

24. Kennedy CE, Fonner VA, O'Reilly KR, Sweat MD. *A systematic review of income generation interventions, including microfinance and vocational skills training, for HIV prevention: AIDS care.* 2014;26(6):659–673.

25. O'Malley TL, Burke JG. A systematic review of microfinance and women's health literature: Directions for future research. *Global Public Health: An International Journal for Research, Policy and Practice.* 2017;12(11): 1433–1460.

26. Fernando G, Durham J, Vlack S, Townsend N, Wickramasinghe K, Gouda H. Examining the evidence of microfinance on non-communicable disease health indicators and outcomes: A systematic literature review. *Global Public Health.* 2022;17(2):165–179.

27. GDi. *Financial Inclusion and Resilience: How BRAC's Microfinance Program Recovered from the West Africa Ebola Crisis.* Global Delivery Initiative; 2017.
28. Pro Mujer. Health care at ProMujer: Going digital to break barriers. 2020.
29. Czura K, Englmaier F, Ho H, Spantig L. Microfinance loan officers before and during Covid-19: Evidence from India. *World Development.* 2022;152: 105812.

Part 4

Conclusion

8 Social finance and health ... new horizon or false dawn?

Introduction

Meeting health and healthcare needs and reducing inequalities in health and well-being are global challenges. As should be clear from the preceding chapters, social finance is not a panacea. Yet it can potentially complement traditional ways of *funding*, and facilitating *access* to, health (care) services and acting on social determinants of health. This book provides the conceptual basis (see Chapters 2–4), and evidence (see Chapters 5–7), for social finance in these roles. While social finance has the ability to act in this way, currently, it does so with differing degrees of success. Nonetheless, exploring the potential role of forms of social finance in responding to specific aspects of global health challenges generates new thinking and evidence relevant to those operating in health systems and social finance and those trying to bridge the gap between them.

This chapter will first present a high-level summary of the main ideas of the book and finish by outlining contributions to two broad areas: new tools for action and impact measurement.

Summary

Conceptual basis

The ability of social finance to play a role in tackling global health challenges stems from its concern with creating social returns and responding to areas of market failure and/or governments focus on efficiency (see Chapter 2). Different forms of social finance do these things in different ways. Chapter 3 outlines the conceptual basis for how impact bonds and microfinance, the main forms of social finance discussed in this book, could play a role in healthcare financing in lower-income countries transitioning to Universal Health Coverage (UHC) and in higher-income countries already with UHC in some form. Microfinance could help shift vulnerable individuals in lower-income countries from exposure to out-of-pocket payments to a form of private (micro)

DOI: 10.4324/9781003305248-12

insurance and, thus, risk-pooling and facilitate less-well-off 'groups' access to health initiatives via microfinance programmes. Through impact bonds, investors could provide up-front funds for the operation of health services to new, or existing, providers paid by the public funder only (i.e. social impact bonds (SIBs)) and directly from foundations, charities or other investors alone or alongside a public funder (i.e. development impact bonds (DIBs)). The former (SIBs) could lead to a more efficient use of funds in countries with UHC that experience pressure on budgets, particularly in challenging economic times, and suffer from rising healthcare costs, as outlays only occur upon meeting agreed outcomes. The latter (DIBs) has the potential to draw more resources into healthcare systems and meet outcomes at the same time. Finally, in Chapter 4, we outline how social finance could act as a determinant of health and well-being. While the mission of microcredit provision and some impact bonds is not explicitly to impact health, each can trigger plausible mechanisms that could lead to health impacts. For example, microcredit could impact employment and income in ways associated with health and well-being. Likewise, aspects of housing and homelessness, which are targeted by interventions via impact bonds, also have similar associations. This conceptualisation provides a new lens through which to view different forms of social finance, opening up the 'evaluative space' when assessing such initiatives.

Evidence

Our mapping review of health impact bonds, in Chapter 5, provides unprecedented insight into their nature and reach in the health system. We identify 58 health impact bonds across 17 countries and categorise them by the level of intervention, delivery mechanisms, policy domain, target population and health indicators. Our findings raise questions about their true nature. Despite claims that impact bonds focus on outcomes and prevention, in general, we find that health impact bonds act further downstream rather than targeting the source of the problem and few focus specifically on outcomes. The former point does not rule out health impact bonds playing a role in health(care) financing. However, the latter point not only makes it difficult to fully assess what role they could play in the health system but raises serious questions about ongoing political and financial support. Although a nascent area of research, the theoretical work and empirical evidence described in Chapter 6 are suggestive of microcredit – through its general use, lending and repayment mechanisms – positively impacting upstream determinants of health. Interestingly, this is the case in both lower- and higher-income countries. This provides a counterpoint to the traditional narrative of the Global South learning from the Global North. Finally, the evidence provided in Chapter 7 suggests that integrated microfinance and health programmes can play a pivotal role in facilitating access to health and healthcare for the most vulnerable and hard-to-reach individuals in lower-income countries. The innovative responses of some microfinance institutions (MFIs) to the COVID-19 pandemic provide a recent and pertinent example of how MFIs enable their clients' access to quality healthcare. Such provision helps fill gaps in health(care) provision and ease pressure on national healthcare budgets while also offering some protection to MFI clients from catastrophic out-of-pocket health (care) payments.

New thinking

New tools for action

Exploring the role of social finance in health is a nascent area of research. Indeed, a motivation for writing this book is awareness raising. We hope the book will provide new tools for action for policymakers, practitioners and researchers working in, and across, healthcare, public health and social finance.

In healthcare, dichotomous debates around the funding and delivery of healthcare traditionally centre on public versus private provision. For the reasons outlined in Chapter 3, we believe that the public sector is best placed to respond to sources of market failure in the financing of healthcare. However, impact bonds and types of microfinance represent interesting examples of hybrid approaches, involving combinations of partnership working between public, private and third sectors, for funding and facilitating access to healthcare. In general, the former being top-down and the latter bottom-up. While these social finance approaches may work imperfectly, they open up the debate about how to journey towards UHC. This is particularly relevant for contexts that lack the infrastructure to collect funds to ensure UHC via taxation.

For public health stakeholders, social finance represents another way of thinking about how to impact health. Microcredit, for example, will not dramatically reduce health inequalities. However, this is beside the point. Evidencing microcredit as a socioeconomic determinant of health again demonstrates the importance of non-health interventions and initiatives for health outcomes. At a minimum, the provision of microcredit illustrates how to avoid inflicting further unnecessary harm on vulnerable individuals through, for example, stress, shame and guilt. More constructively, there is scope for debt to be a positive experience that contributes to, for example, increases in confidence, control, feelings of self-worth and social participation. While further exploration and evidencing of these links is necessary, initial findings are given further strength through complementary work exploring how social enterprises, more generally, impact health and well-being, despite this not being an explicit objective (1). Taken together, this body of work illustrates the importance of not just *what* you do but *how* you do it. Consequently, a more general take-away is around the delivery of interventions, products and services being as worthy of consideration for impacting on determinants of health as the good itself.

In the social finance sector, there are benefits for different stakeholders, including practitioners and researchers. For microfinance practitioners, evidencing how their institutions positively impact (determinants of) health adds to the case for regulation, and public sector funding, designed to strengthen and develop these alternative economic spaces. This is particularly relevant for those institutions operating in contexts that cannot benefit from economies of scale; the provision of microcredit in the UK being an exemplar. Such lenders already respond to market failures by operating in areas vacated by private sector institutions that cannot generate a profit. However, the relatively high transaction costs of offering microloans and the relatively small size of the market available further impede their ability to operate sustainably. For impact bond practitioners, as previously stated, it is vital that payments are tied to outcomes. This is their raison d'etre. Failure to do so raises questions about the legitimacy of the project. For social finance researchers, there is the opportunity to explore the role of other forms of social finance in responding to aspects of global health challenges. We purposively selected those forms of social finance – microfinance and impact bonds – with the relatively most well-developed theory and evidence in relation to health. However, this is not to say that other forms of social finance, such as venture philanthropy or crowdfunding, could, or already do, respond to health challenges in similar, or indeed new, ways.

Finally, for policymakers more generally, exploring and evidencing the links between social finance and health further highlights the importance of taking a joined-up or intersectoral approach to health policymaking. As outlined in Chapter 4, one well-known approach is Health in All Policies (HiAP). However, HiAP is challenging, requiring political will to facilitate cooperation across sectors. This could be particularly contentious, as resource shifts across sectors may be necessary. Yet, as the potential of social finance illustrates, taking an intersectoral approach could help overcome policy silos for acting on, and indeed funding, and facilitating, access to health(care) services.

Rethinking how to measure impact

A thread running through this book is the importance of measuring impact. As outlined in Chapter 6, in the field of impact evaluation for social and development interventions, randomised controlled trials (RCTs) are often portrayed as the gold standard for their ability to deal with the attribution problem and selection biases. They gain further credence from their association with the medical field where the rigour of impact evaluation is enviously viewed from the social sciences. Their use has proliferated within the microfinance sector since the first microcredit RCT in 2005 and they are also frequently used to evaluate impact bonds (2–4). Well-known critiques exist, including: RCTs being silent about how and why an effect has occurred (commonly referred to as a 'black box' approach to evaluation); their resource intensiveness (in terms of cost and time); not always being ethically possible to undertake; and focusing on average, rather than distributional, effects (5–7). One further critique is the risk of underestimating the impact of complex interventions, of the sort found within social finance, by taking a blinkered approach to evaluation.

Interventions are deemed complex when the health pathways and intervention mechanisms through which health impacts occur are numerous and interacting. Therefore, some forms of microfinance and the interventions funded via impact bonds, of the types described in Chapters 5–7, are complex health interventions; for example, aiming to impact health through microcredit and well-being via impact bond-funded unemployment or education interventions. In the UK, the Medical Research Council (MRC) guidelines on developing and evaluating complex interventions ask researchers to reflect on whether an RCT is the most appropriate study design for their intended purpose and recognise the value of alternative research designs (8). This is important for those working in both the microfinance and impact bond sectors. We know that not all borrowers engaging with microcredit are affected the same way and that RCTs may have underestimated the impact of microfinance (9–11). The fallout of underestimating impact is arguably even greater within the impact bond sector as payments are tied to meeting outcomes; statistical concepts could risk obfuscating the diversity of impact. In the preceding chapters, we have purposively highlighted the value of using alternative methods to explore impact, such as financial diaries and qualitative methods. There is a need for those working in social finance to embrace alternative methods. One such underutilised approach in social finance is realist methods.

Realist methods are concerned with the question of what works, for whom, in which circumstances and why (12). The value of this approach is from moving beyond 'what works,' which is the typical focus of RCTs, to also generate insight into how and why impact occurs. This means that, unlike RCTs that have limited generalisability, realist approaches are better equipped to generate insights that are transferrable to different contexts (13,14). These methods speak to concerns within the MRC guidelines by generating insight into whether and how interventions work for different people in different contexts and are gaining momentum in public health. While there is a place for RCTs, being fixated on this approach risks those within the social finance sector again failing to keep pace with alternative and cutting-edge approaches embraced by those working in public health.

Conclusion

The challenge of meeting healthcare needs and the persistence and growth of health inequalities, both globally and within countries, require new solutions. We propose and critically explore the role of social finance not only in *funding* and facilitating *access* to health(care) services, but also in *acting on* the social determinants of health. By doing so, we hope to open up the conversation about how forms of social finance could complement their more traditional publicly financed and public health counterparts, leading to health creation in ways not often recognised. While social finance acts imperfectly in these roles, the process of exploration has generated new tools for action for policymakers, practitioners and researchers working in, and across, healthcare, public health and social finance and contributed to the debates around impact measurement. Social finance is a nascent area of policy and practice. Many have claimed it to be transformational. But, like many such claims with respect to other initiatives, it is safer to say it has a place. With more research and evidence to come, much more remains to be said about the magnitude of that place and the directions in which it moves. We hope the book will stimulate further discussions not only about new ways from within social finance, and elsewhere, to respond to global health challenges, but also further research to bridge the gap between rhetoric and reality in this exciting field.

References

1. Roy M, Farmer J. *Social Enterprise, Health, and Wellbeing: Theory, Methods, and Practice*. Routledge; 2021.
2. Albertson K, Bailey C, Fox J, LaBarbera C, O'Leary C, Painter G. *Payment by Results and Social Impact Bonds: Outcome-Based Payment Systems in the UK and US*. Bristol: Policy Press; 2018.
3. Hulse ESG, Atun R, McPake B, Lee JT. Use of social impact bonds in financing health systems responses to non-communicable diseases: Scoping review. *BMJ Global Health*. 2021;6(3):e004127.
4. Banerjee A, Duflo E, Glennerster R, Kinnan C. The miracle of microfinance? Evidence from a randomized evaluation. *American Economic Journal: Applied Economics*. 2015;7(1):22–53.
5. Bédécarrats F, Guérin I, Roubaud F, editors. Editors' Introduction: Controversies around RCT in Development: Epistemology, Ethics, and

Politics. In: *Randomized Control Trials in the Field of Development*. 1st ed. Oxford: Oxford University Press; 2020.

6. Bédécarrats F, Guérin I, Morvant-Roux S, Roubaud F. Behind the scenes of science in action: A 'replication in context' of a randomised control trial in Morocco. *Third World Quarterly*. 2021;42(11):2669–2689.

7. McHugh N, Biosca O, Donaldson C. From wealth to health: Evaluating microfinance as a complex intervention. *Evaluation*. 2017;23(2):209–225.

8. Skivington K, Matthews L, Simpson SA, Craig P, Baird J, Blazeby JM, et al. A new framework for developing and evaluating complex interventions: Update of Medical Research Council guidance. *BMJ*. 2021;n2061.

9. Banerjee A, Karlan D, Zinman J. Six randomized evaluations of microcredit: Introduction and further steps. *American Economic Journal: Applied Economics*. 2015;7(1):1–21.

10. Dahal M, Fiala N. What do we know about the impact of microfinance? The problems of statistical power and precision. *World Development*. 2020;128: 104773.

11. Breza E, Kinnan C. Measuring the equilibrium impacts of credit: Evidence from the Indian microfinance crisis. *The Quarterly Journal of Economics*. 2021;136(3):1447–1497.

12. Pawson R, Tilley N. *Realistic Evaluation*. SAGE Publications Ltd; 1997.

13. Astbury B. Making Claims Using Realist Methods. In: *Doing Realist Research*. Los Angeles: SAGE Publications Ltd; 2018. pp. 59–78.

14. Meager R. Understanding the average impact of microcredit expansions: A Bayesian hierarchical analysis of seven randomized experiments. *American Economic Journal: Applied Economics*. 2019;11(1):57–91.

Index

Note: **Bold** page numbers refer to tables and *italic* page numbers refer to figures.